Communication Policy and Planning in Singapore

by

Eddie C. Y. Kuo
Peter S. J. Chen

Kegan Paul International
London, Boston and Melbourne

in association with
East-West Communication Institute
Honolulu

First published in 1983
by Kegan Paul International
39 Store Street, London WC1E 7DD, England
9 Park Street, Boston, Mass. 02108, USA
296 Beaconsfield Parade, Middle Park,
Melbourne, 3206, Australia
Printed in Great Britain by
The Thetford Press Ltd., Thetford, Norfolk

ISBN 0-7103-0064-6

Table of Contents

Foreword

This study is an outcome of a research activity organized by the Communication Policy and Planning Project, East-West Communication Institute, Honolulu, Hawaii.

A small team of researchers from the United States, the Philippines, Singapore, Thailand, Bangladesh, and Sri Lanka met at EWCI in April 1977 and prepared a research design for a series of case studies on communication policy and planning. After conducting fieldwork in their respective countries, the group of researchers returned to EWCI in April 1978 to analyze data and prepare reports. The initial reports were then presented in a seminar attended by 20 communication policymakers, planners, and managers from the United States and ten Asian and Pacific countries.

The exchange of ideas and views between the researchers and EWCI staff and the teamwork carried out at various stages, contributed significantly toward the development of the case studies.

In this study, Dr. Eddie Kuo and Dr. Peter Chen (who are sociologists by training) have provided an overview of the Singapore society and its communication systems. After providing the context, they have examined the main aspects of communication policy in Singapore. Finally, they have examined in some detail, communication planning at the Radio and Television Singapore and the Singapore Family Planning and Population Board.

The case study introduces the reader into the very complex and unresearched area of communication policy and planning in an Asian country. Its main contribution is in providing a framework highlighting the essential elements of communication policymaking and planning for social development in Singapore. It gives a base from which more in-depth research studies into the contents of specific policies and the complex process of policymaking can be undertaken.

Syed A. Rahim
Project Leader

1

Introduction

Communication policy and planning is emerging as a new area of study that has attracted the attention of many communication researchers and institutions. Because it is a relatively young and unexplored field, and because of the "pragmatic" nature of policy research, the study of communication policy and planning is in great need of empirical case studies, through which the substance of policies and the factors and mechanisms involved in their formulation and implementation may be identified.

The present study arises from an effort to analyze communication policy and planning in the society of Singapore, with a special focus on communication activities in relation to social development in this island-republic.

Singapore—the smallest yet most developed nation in Southeast Asia—celebrated its thirteenth anniversary as an independent state in 1978 with confidence in its viability as a physical and political entity. Since its separation from the Federation of Malaysia in 1965, the republic has maintained constant high economic growth rates and pursued a path of social development that has produced encouraging signs of the emergence of a Singapore identity. Such achievements in economic resilience, political stability, and social cohesion are impressive when considered in relation to the extent of cultural and ethnic diversity and the lack of natural resources in Singapore.

A student in communication will not fail to notice the presence of communication barriers in Singapore. The population is composed of three major ethnic groups: Chinese, Malay, and Indian. Religious affiliation is similarly heterogeneous with each of the major religions of the world well represented. The most direct and obvious barrier to communication comes from the complex linguistic diversity in the island-state, where a handful of major languages coexist. Therefore, while the people of Singapore have no doubt been brought under the same political and economic systems, sharing the same destiny, there is legitimate concern whether they have been effectively tied together under the same communication network. The questions that concern us as communication researchers are:

1. How and to what extent has a national communication network been

established in Singapore to serve the diversified population and to help achieve the goals of national development?
2. What are the guiding policies, adopted by the government and political leaders, that serve to direct and constrain the operation of the communication network in Singapore?
3. What factors and processes influence communication planning in Singapore?
4. How do the leaders of Singapore utilize communication resources to mobilize the population to participate in national programs for social development?

Judging from the social and economic accomplishments of Singapore during its short history against such social-cultural constraints, these are problems of both theoretical and applied import that deserve careful and systematic study.

Objectives

A review of literature reveals that, except for some theses on the history of various language presses (Kanayson 1956; Burns 1957; M. Chen 1967), there has been little research done in Singapore on the communication network and its components. Similarly, of the few publications on policy planning and decision-making processes publicly available in Singapore, most are concerned with either urban planning, economic planning, or family planning. The present study on communication policy and planning, being the first of its kind in Singapore, is an attempt to explore and analyze the following areas:

1. Communication Systems: We purport to have made a thorough investigation of the existing communication network and its major components in Singapore. The component systems discussed include the press and other print media, radio, television, cinema, postal service, and telecommunications.
2. Communication Policy: The guiding national communication policies and legal and regulatory constraints in operation in Singapore today are identified and described. Following the definition of Unesco, communication policies are seen as sets of social norms "established to guide the behavior of communication systems" (quoted in Rahim 1977, p. 13). Such policies are identified from statements made by political leaders who are directly responsible for the legislation of legal codes and their implementation as it pertains to the working of communication systems. The legal constraints directly or indirectly related to communication activities are therefore operational means of translating the guiding policies into forces directing or constraining the operation of communication systems.
3. National Level Policy Planning: Since in Singapore there is no cen-

tralized agency responsible for overall communication planning, planning processes at the national level can be assessed only by aggregating piecemeal planning efforts within various ministries or statutory boards that happen to include communication elements. Such processes are analyzed within the context of overall policy planning at the national level. Most such communication planning involves the development of communication facilities or infrastructure.

4. Institutional Level Communication Planning: To understand how the processes and dynamics of policy formulation and planning apply to communication, a study of communication planning at the institutional level is necessary. The institution chosen for such a case study is Radio Television Singapore—probably the most popular and influential communication organ supporting the goals of social development in Singapore.
5. Project Level Communication Planning: Singapore is well known for its effective and constant mass campaigns, which promote development objectives by effecting attitudinal and behavioral changes in the population. (Better known campaign slogans are "Keep Singapore Clean," "Use Your Hand," and "Girl or Boy, Two is Enough.") An analysis of the use of communication resources in relation to the propagation of campaign messages in Singapore can provide important lessons on the supportive function of the communication system. We focus on family planning campaigns in Singapore to illustrate how a government organization (Singapore Family Planning and Population Board) pools national communication resources to diffuse the norms and practices of family planning in Singapore.

Methodology

As a comprehensive case study of communication policy and planning in Singapore, the present research draws data from various sources in order to give an overall picture. The main sources of data were:

1. Documentary materials: These have been used extensively to describe communication systems and analyze the formulation and emergence of communication policies. Major documents used included parliamentary debate records, addresses of political leaders, reports of government and nongovernment institutions, legal statutes, government statistics, and newspapers.
2. Personal interviews with communication practitioners, government officials, and community leaders: The interviews were unstructured in order to obtain an inside view of communication systems and their operational processes. Fieldwork assistants were asked to prepare field study notes as participant observers in various capacities.
3. Media survey data: Data from a media survey have been used to describe the extent of media exposure and the relative functionality of various

media as perceived by the population. The survey on "Media Habits and Information Needs in Singapore" was sponsored by the Asian Mass Communication Information and Research Center (AMIC) and carried out by authors of this report. The study which was completed in late 1977, used a quota sample of 612 Singaporeans aged 15 and above (controlled for sex, ethnicity, working status, and housing type).

Organization of the Report

This report consists of nine chapters, including this introduction. In chapter 2, the socio-demographic characteristics of Singapore society are discussed and the history, politics, government, and economy are sketched. The chapter provides a general background for understanding better how communication policies were formed and implemented as well as how communication systems developed in Singapore.

In chapter 3, the component systems of the communication network in Singapore today are described. The systems analyzed include the press and other print media, broadcasting media (radio, television, and Rediffusion), cinemas and films, postal services, and telecommunications (telephone, telex, telegraph, and satellite communication.)

The next chapter (chapter 4) contains an audience analysis covering the use of major types of mass media by the population broken down by demographic characteristics such as ethnicity, age, and sex. The perceived usefulness of these media in fulfilling the information needs of the population is also discussed.

Chapter 5 deals with the guiding communication policies on which the present communication systems are built and operated. The legal and regulatory constraints that direct and control the operation of several communication systems are presented in detail. The rationales behind the policies are discussed, as well as their possible consequences.

Chapter 6 is focused on the structure of general policymaking and planning at the national level in Singapore. Strategies and agencies of development planning and urban planning are discussed in some detail. At the national level of communication planning, agencies involved with the planning of certain communication elements are identified.

In chapter 7, communication planning at the institutional level is the topic, using Radio Television Singapore (RTS) as a case study. The structure and operation of RTS are presented, together with its role in support of development objectives.

In chapter 8, the focus is shifted from institutional level planning to project level planning. The communication activities of the Singapore Family Planning and Population Board are analyzed in detail to illustrate the use of promotional media, along with general organizational support, in one of the most successful family planning programs in the world.

Chapter 9 concludes the report with a summary and some generalizations on communication policy and planning in Singapore.

2

Singapore Society

Singapore is an island situated at the tip of the Malay Peninsula, with a land area of approximately 616 square kilometers. The island is linked physically to the Malay Peninsula by a three-quarter mile causeway carrying a road and a railway. As a small island-republic, Singapore has few natural resources. The only ones it possesses are its deep-water harbor and its strategic location at the crossroads of Southeast Asia, where major shipping and transportation routes between the Pacific Ocean and the Indian Ocean intersect. It was this strategic position that attracted the attention of Sir Stamford Raffles in 1819 when he decided to establish a port here to protect the trade interests of the British East India Company. Today, Singapore continues to rely on its strategic position for its economic survival.

History

Soon after its inception in 1819, the position of Singapore as the chief British colony in the area was consolidated, in 1832, when Singapore was made the center of government for the Straits Settlements, including Penang and Malacca, as an extension of British India. During the next hundred years, with the opening of the Suez Canal and the strengthening of Britain-China trade, Singapore's importance as a seaport and trading post increased. Over the years, Singapore grew steadily in size and importance until 1942, when British rule was interrupted by Japan.

On February 15, 1942, the Japanese invaded the island. For the next three and a half years, Singapore was renamed Syonan, or Shonan, under the Japanese rule. The Allied Forces led by Lord Louis Mountbatten regained the island in September 1945 and reinstituted British rule under the British Military Administration.

On April 1, 1946, civil government was established in Singapore. As a political unit, the Straits Settlements was dissolved, with Penang and Malacca joining the Malay Union (later the Federation of Malaya) in 1948. In the following years, political developments both inside and outside of Singapore led to full internal self-government in 1959. Singapore became an independent state with a constitution which gave the island complete internal self-government with the British controlling defense and foreign affairs.

Finally, Singapore became fully independent of British colonial rule by joining the Federation of Malaysia on September 16, 1963. The marriage, however, was short-lived and ill-fated. With political struggles and communal tension reaching dangerous points following the merger, the Malaysian government under Tengku Abdul Rahman unilaterally announced the separation of Singapore from the Federation of Malaysia on August 9, 1965, causing Singapore to become a new independent state—the youngest and the smallest in the region.

Socio-Demographic Characteristics

Since the early 19th century, Singapore has grown from a small village of a few hundred inhabitants to a modern metropolitan city of over 2.3 million people. Each influx of immigrants in the past 160 years has added to the ethnic complexity of the island. The population of Singapore is composed of about 76 percent Chinese, 15 percent Malays, 7 percent Indians (a census category including Pakistanis and Ceylonese), and 2 percent from other ethnic origins including Europeans, Eurasians, and others.

The ethnic heterogeneity of Singapore's population is paralleled by its linguistic diversity. Each of the three major ethnic communities contains a number of dialect speech groups. As a compromise among the three major ethnic communities, the leaders of Singapore decided at the time of independence that there would be four official languages in the new republic. Malay, Chinese (Mandarin), and Tamil were selected to represent the three ethnic-cultural traditions in Singapore, plus English because of its international status and Singapore's colonial background. Of the four, Malay was designated the national language, a reflection of both the history and the geographical position of the island-state. Today, however, the role of the national language is more ceremonial than functional. The *de facto* dominant working language is English. (See Kuo 1976; 1977a.)

Government and Politics

The political situation in post-colonial Singapore is dominated by the People's Action Party (PAP). Since the PAP's rise to power in the 1959 election, when it gained 43 of the 51 seats, the PAP has dominated Singapore's parliament, and its leader, Mr. Lee Kuan Yew, has served as prime minister (PM) from that time. Since 1968, despite subsequent elections in 1972 and 1976, the PAP has been the only political party represented in parliament.

Singapore is governed as a parliamentary democracy with a president at its head. Parliament, which is unicameral, consists of 69 members elected by the population in single-member constituencies. Voting age in Singapore is 21, and voting in elections is compulsory. Parliament is presided over by a speaker who may or may not be an elected member. Debates and discussions in parliament may be conducted in any one of the four official languages; simultaneous interpretation is provided. Votes and proceedings, as well as the official reports of parliament, are in English.

The president of the republic is elected by parliament for a term of four years. The prime minister, who must be a member of parliament and command the support of a majority of its members, is appointed by the president. The other ministers are also appointed by the president, who, acting on the advice of the prime minister, selects from among members of parliament.

The cabinet, presided over by the prime minister, controls the government and is collectively responsible to parliament for policy. Meetings are held in secret, to discuss all important points of departmental policies and to decide the appropriate action. The cabinet is composed of the prime minister and ministers holding the portfolios in communication, culture, defense, education, the environment, finance, foreign affairs, health, home affairs, labor, law, national development, science and technology, and social affairs. The cabinet ministers, who are no doubt drawn from the ruling political elites, direct the implementation of policies by civil bureaucrats in departments under each ministry. A number of statutory bodies have also been created in Singapore's government structure to articulate particular activities and provide greater effectiveness in the implementation and coordination of development programs.

According to an analysis by P. Chen (1978), the political elite and the leading civil servants operate in a tight and efficient partnership. The politicians set up the goals and objectives of the development plan, and the bureaucrats implement. The power elite is described as a "strong, cohesive and homogeneous" group whose members follow the same line of political thinking and maintain the same interests and objectives.

The same observation is made by a local political scientist:

> The division between the administrator and the politician is particularly blurred because it is unstated official policy to politicize the administrators and to entrust them with major power in decision making in the government enterprises. (Chan 1975, p. 63)

With political stability maintained through the dominance of PAP, and without the existence of any viable and accountable opposition groups in the past ten years, the meaningful political arena in Singapore is shifting. According to Chan (1975, p. 51), "One of the most significant developments in Singapore politics in the last decade has been the steady and systematic depoliticization of a politically active and aggressive citizenry." The result is the emergence of an administrative state with a depoliticized population. Economics is in the limelight, not politics.

Economy

Lacking natural resources, and having a small land area and a high density of population, Singapore has always depended on its central location at the intersection of major trade routes and its great natural harbor for economic survival. The entrepôt trade has been and continues to be a major component in Singapore's economic strength. Yet, with self-government in 1959, when the ruling People's Action Party assumed power, it became clear that Singapore must industrialize and broaden its economic base to provide sufficient employment opportunities for its growing population. The government launched a massive industrialization program with the goals of establishing a viable manufacturing sector, and creating trained manpower and an infrastructure for further economic development.

Today, manufacturing has become the most dynamic sector in the Singapore economy, accounting for about a quarter of the Gross Domestic Product. Singapore has also become one of the largest oil refining centers of the world and operates the world's fourth busiest port, after Rotterdam, New York, and Yokohama. Its capacities for ship building and repair have also expanded greatly, ranking twenty-first in the world in the former.

During the period of transition since the early 1960s and to a great extent during the period of expansion since 1971, it has been the policy of the government to participate directly in the development of Singapore's economy. The participation is most obvious in the attraction of foreign capital investments, the creation of the necessary infrastructure, and direct government investment in projects. The objectives are clearly to develop Singapore as a center for financial services as well as the trade center of the Southeast Asian region, and to create a diversified industrial economy with increasing emphasis on technology-intensive activities. Economically and technologically, Singapore is pushing further as a "global city" to serve the region and the world.

This is most vividly described by the Foreign Minister, Mr. S. Rajaratnam:

> Once you see Singapore as a Global City, the problem of hinterland becomes unimportant because for a Global City the world is its hinterland. . . . An independent Singapore survives and will survive because it has established a relationship of interdependence in the rapidly [expanding] global economic system. Singapore's economic future will, as the years go by, become more and more rooted in this global system. (*The Mirror,* February 14, 1972)

3

Components of Communication Systems

The Press

Singapore is served by 11 daily newspapers, of which 3 are published in English, 4 in Chinese, 1 in Malay (Rumi script), 2 in Tamil and 1 in Malayalam (Table 1). Daily newspapers in all four official languages are therefore available, serving the ethnically and linguistically diversified population. The total daily newspaper circulation (not including Sunday papers) was estimated to be 477,000 in 1976. (See Table 3.) This gives a circulation rate of 209 papers per 1,000 population, making Singapore among the highest in the region. The figure is also consistent with the statistics cited by Feliciano in Table 2.

The newspaper with the longest history and the largest circulation is the English-language *Straits Times* which claimed to sell more than 144,000 copies daily in 1976. The other English-language papers are the *New Nation,* an afternoon paper focusing more on entertainment and sports news, and the *Business Times,* the latest to enter the field (in late 1976) with the

Table 1

Daily Newspapers in Singapore

Name	Year Started	Language
Berita Harian	1957	Malay
Business Times	1976	English
Malaysian Malayali	1938	Malayalam
Min Pao	1961	Chinese
Nanyang Siang Pau	1923	Chinese
New Nation	1971	English
Shin Min Daily	1967	Chinese
Sin Chew Jit Poh	1929	Chinese
Straits Times	1845	English
Tamil Malar	1964	Tamil
Tamil Marasu	1934	Tamil

Table 2

Newspaper Circulation Rate in Southeast Asian Countries

Country	Newspaper Circulation Rate (per 1,000 population)
Laos	6
Indonesia	7
Burma	9
Cambodia	22
Thailand	24
Philippines	35
South Vietnam	67
Malaysia	74
Singapore	201
Hong Kong	485

Source: *Asian Press & Media Directory*, 1974, quoted in Feliciano, 1976, p. 191; statistics refer to various years.

business circle as its main readership target. All three English-language dailies, as well as the two very popular Sunday papers, the *Sunday Times* and the *Sunday Nation*, belong to the powerful Straits Times Press Ltd.

Chinese-language dailies are more numerous and enjoy a large circulation in Singapore. Competition among them is more genuine. *Nanyang Siang Pau* and *Sin Chew Jit Poh* both enjoy wide circulation and are serious and informative in their coverage. The *Shin Min Daily* and *Min Pao* are much smaller in circulation and more sensational in coverage.

The only Malay-language newspaper is *Berita Harian* which is also part of the *Straits Times* group. It serves the Malay community with a circulation of about 28,000. The two Tamil-language dailies, *Tamil Murasu* and *Tamil Malar*, are small in circulation with a combined circulation of about 7,100 in 1976. The only nonofficial language daily, *Malaysian Malayali*, is a small paper supported by a circulation of 800 in 1976; it serves the older, first-generation Malayalam native-speakers in both Singapore and Malaysia. As a vernacular paper without support from educational and other social institutions, this paper has an uncertain future.

Comparison of circulation figures since 1973 (Table 3) shows that the Chinese-language dailies have been, up to 1976, the most widely circulated of all, although their share of total circulation has declined in recent years. In contrast, the English papers are gaining in both total circulation and proportion. With the addition of a new English-language daily, *Business Times*, there is good reason to expect that the total circulation of the English-language papers has exceeded that of the Chinese today. Both Malay and Tamil dailies are small in circulation, capturing less than 8 percent of the overall circulation.

Table 3

Daily Newspaper Circulation by Language, 1973-1976

Language	Number of Newspapers	1973 N	1973 %	1974 N	1974 %	1975 N	1975 %	1976 N	1976 %
Chinese	4	252,487	57.2	223,300	52.9	227,400	50.8	235,200	49.3
English	2*	161,479	36.5	168,000	39.8	186,600	41.7	206,000	43.2
Malay (Rumi)	1	19,989	4.5	23,300	5.5	26,300	5.9	27,900	5.8
Tamil	2							7,100	1.5
		7,851	1.8	7,900	1.9	7,700	1.7		
Malayalam	1							800	0.2
Total	10*	441,806	100.0	422,500	100.0	448,000	100.0	477,000	100.0

Source: Computed from *Singapore Facts and Pictures*, Singapore: The Publicity Division, Ministry of Culture, 1975, p. 151; 1976, p. 175; 1977, p. 183.

*A new English language daily, *Business Times*, was inaugurated in late 1976, increasing the total number of English language dailies to 3, and making 11 dailies altogether.

Different language newspapers in Singapore have distinctive cultural and journalistic traditions. The English-language papers serve all three ethnic communities and are thus supraethnic in outlook. Their circulations have been increasing steadily. This trend is expected to continue and is consistent with the increasing status of the English language in Singapore (see Kuo 1977a and 1978). Daily newspapers in other official languages (Chinese, Malay, and Tamil) cater mainly to their respective ethnic communities. They therefore publish articles of both general interest and particular communal interest. For instance, Chinese newspapers publish articles about clan association meetings and social functions, while the Malay and Tamil papers likewise pay special attention to activities of Muslim groups or Indian organizations in Singapore.

In a content analysis of news articles in Singapore, Lim, Lui-Tan and Foo (1975) compared the newspaper contents of the leading English-language paper, *Straits Times,* and one of the leading Chinese-language papers, *Nanyang Siang Pau*. The following findings, though tentative because of the small sample involved, suggest the general nature of contents of newspapers in Singapore:

1. Source of news: Local news ranks highest in both papers, followed by news from Asia, then that from outside Asia. The *Straits Times* has a substantially higher amount of news from outside Asia than *Nanyang Siang Pau*, mainly because the former uses more syndicated feature articles from overseas.
2. Political and economic news from outside Singapore ranks fairly high in both papers, reflecting the Republic's heavy dependence on regional and international activities and its need to be well informed.
3. At the local level, Singapore papers give higher priority to social and community news than to political news. This is especially true for *Nanyang Siang Pau*.

4. Neither paper is sensational in nature, although the emphasis on sports is high.

Lim and her colleagues concluded that "the English paper performs more of an informational function and the Chinese gives almost equal emphasis to education and information."

There are three major journalists' groups in Singapore. The most important is the Singapore National Union of Journalists (SNUJ), with members from different language papers. The SNUJ functions as a trade union looking after labor conditions in the journalism industry. Occasionally, it also organizes seminars and speeches on topics related to journalism. The second group is the Singapore Press Club, composed mainly of journalists from the English papers, foreign news correspondents, advertising executives, and public relations people from business companies. It is primarily a social club with members meeting regularly over lunch, sometimes with speakers on current issues. Third is the Chinese Press Club (Paolin Club) with more than two hundred members from the Chinese newspapers and the Chinese news division of Radio Television Singapore. Regular social and professional activities are organized by this club.

Other Print Media

Two factors inhibit the development of the printing industry in Singapore: One is the small population, which limits the size of the market, and the other, which further complicates it, is the linguistic diversity of the reading public. Although the literacy rate in Singapore is estimated to be around 75-80 percent (72 percent in 1970)—which means up to 80 percent of the population aged 10 years and over can read in one of the four official languages—the percentage of those who can read a *given* official language is much lower (cf. Kuo 1974). Publications in any given language can therefore reach only a segment of the population. Furthermore, local publications have to compete with publications imported into Singapore—English-language publications from Britain, the United States, and Australia; Chinese-language publications from Hong Kong and Taiwan; and Malay-language ones from Malaysia and Indonesia.

Considering these difficulties, the printing industry in Singapore has fared quite well in its development and expansion over the years. According to official statistics (*The Mirror,* September 12, 1977), there were in 1977 a total of 207 printing establishments of 10 or more workers, providing employment to some 8,500 persons, or 4 percent of the manufacturing work force in Singapore. Of these printing firms, however, only 13 were large companies with 100 or more workers and an output valued at more than $1 million per annum. This reflects the dominance of a small number of printing companies in the industry. In 1975, the total annual output of the industry was $255 million. Significantly about 20 percent of this output, consisting mainly of books and pamphlets, was for export (*The Mirror*, September 12, 1977). With a small, competitive domestic market that is close to being saturated, the future of Singapore's printing industry seems to lie in the expansion of its overseas market. This is being explored with the encouragement and support of the government.

Numerous foreign publications flow into Singapore. Yet, as pointed out by Lim, Lui-Tan and Foo (1975), the print media are the only media that can claim to offset some of this inflow by the export of books to other countries. Of those exported, a large proportion are locally produced textbooks used in neighboring countries. The picture is reversed when it comes to imported magazines and journals (Lim, Lui-Tan and Foo 1975, p. 17). News weeklies and popular magazines, such as *Time*, *Newsweek*, and *Reader's Digest*, as well as women's magazines and comic books, are available at local newsstands.

Book related activities in Singapore are actively promoted by the National Library and several organizations, such as the National Book Development Council (founded 1969), the Library Association of Singapore (founded 1955), the Singapore Booksellers' Association (founded 1968), and the Master Printers' Association (founded 1937).

The National Library of Singapore has an important role in relation to the print media. By an act of parliament, the National Library is empowered to collect and receive all materials printed and published in Singapore, thus ensuring a permanent record of indigenous works. It advises on and coordinates the resources and services of government department libraries with its own resources, and provides reference, bibliographic, and inter-library loan services to government departments and to parliament. In addition, it acts as the organizing agency for national and international lending and exchange of materials. The National Library is also a public library that provides reference and loan services to people in Singapore. At the end of December 1977, the library had a membership of 341,288—about 14.7 percent of the population. Most of the members are young people under 20 years of age (*The Mirror*, April 3, 1978). The expanding membership of the National Library from 1966 to 1976 is shown in Table 4.

The book collection of the National Library at the end of September 1977 numbered 1,035,281 (*The Mirror*, April 3, 1978). Books in all four official languages are collected. Other collections include bound periodicals, music sheets and orchestral scores, microfilms, braille books, microfiches, maps, prints, gramophone records, talking books, films, filmstrips, tapes, and slides. The increase in book collection over the years in each of the four official languages since 1966 is presented in Table 5.

The National Library has two full-time branch libraries, two part-time branch libraries, and ten mobile libraries deployed at designated community centers. The National Library plans to build more full-time branch libraries in accordance with its decentralization policy, and will gradually phase out the mobile library service (*The Mirror*, April 3, 1978).

Table 4

National Library Membership, 1966–1976

Year	Total	Persons Aged 15 and Over	Children Under 15
1966	119,643	30,468	89,175
1967	129,039	36,422	92,617
1968	145,196	43,156	102,040
1969	157,398	50,047	107,351
1970	177,513	60,022	117,491
1971	198,493	69,724	128,769
1972	218,684	79,555	139,129
1973	236,967	93,270	143,697
1974	275,984	112,639	163,345
1975	296,299	129,457	166,842
1976	319,847	146,993	172,854

Source: Department of Statistics, 1977, p. 230.

Radio and Television

The Broadcasting and Television Act of 1963, empowers the government with the exclusive privilege of establishing and operating radio and television stations in Singapore. Administratively, Radio Television Singapore (RTS) under the Ministry of Culture is responsible for broadcasting services.[1] As a government institution, RTS is entrusted "with the responsibility of interpreting the long-term objectives and policies of the Government, and particularly in maintaining a sense of national identity" (Ministry of Culture 1973).

Radio broadcasting in Singapore dates from 1935 under the British-Malaya Broadcasting Corporation (BMBC), a private commercial enterprise. Over the years, the broadcasting system changed from a private commercial operation to a quasi-government operation and finally a wholly government organization. Presently, Radio Singapore broadcasts four separate language channels plus an FM stereo service and a shortwave service for overseas listeners. Each of the four major channels goes on the air for about 16 to 19 hours daily between 5:00 a.m. and midnight. The total air time on AM channels averages 504 hours per week.

Television was introduced in Singapore on February 15, 1963, when a pilot daily service of 1½ hours on a single channel was inaugurated. The hours of transmission on this channel were gradually extended, and in November 1963, a second channel was put in service. Color television was introduced in 1974, and the programs are now almost completely in color.

[1]RTS was reorganized as the Singapore Broadcasting Corporation (SBC) in early 1980 under the Singapore Broadcasting Corporation Bill (1980), thus becoming an independent statutory board. While no changes in the basic broadcasting policy are expected, the implications of the reorganization remain to be seen.

Table 5

Books at the National Library by Language, 1966-1976

Year	Total	Language			
		Malay	Chinese	Indian	English
1966	286,000	33,500	65,500	18,000	169,000
1967	317,100	41,200	71,700	20,400	183,800
1968	379,900	48,900	99,500	25,000	206,500
1969	426,100	55,700	110,400	30,200	229,800
1970	460,552	56,299	124,946	33,259	246,048
1971	520,280	66,363	139,922	38,422	275,573
1972	585,097	77,371	153,532	43,916	310,278
1973	702,696	90,238	195,915	57,537	359,006
1974	784,660	103,777	224,518	61,841	394,524
1975	877,207	116,603	254,537	69,849	436,218
1976	971,717	129,020	283,792	70,379	488,526

Source: Department of Statistics, 1977, p. 229.

Today, Television Singapore operates two channels, telecasting a total of over 100 hours of programs per week. Transmission is in all four official languages and several Chinese dialects. (It is clear that present policy is to gradually phase out programs in dialects.) Subtitles are incorporated extensively, using English or Malay subtitles for Chinese or Indian programs, or vice versa.

A license is required to operate radio and television sets at a given premise in Singapore. In 1976, there were a total of 60,148 radio licenses and 309,276 television licenses which also permit the use of radio sets (see Table 6). Since each license allows the use of one or more sets at a premise, it is not possible to estimate the total number of radio and television sets in use in Singapore. According to Far Eastern Economic Review's *Asia 1976 Yearbook*, there were 320 radio sets per 1,000 population in Singapore (in contrast to 14 in Indonesia, 83 in Thailand, 46 in the Philippines, and 42 in Malaysia) and 252.2 television receivers per 1,000 population in Singapore (in contrast to 20 for the Philippines and 2.3 for Indonesia). In making this comparison, it should also be pointed out that Singapore is a metropolitan urban center that naturally involves more communication activities and provides higher media exposure for its population. However, a comparison between Singapore and other urban centers in Southeast Asia will not be possible until relevant data is available.

In addition to the two channels provided by Television Singapore, people in Singapore can tune in to two channels from Television Malaysia that provide only black and white programs, mostly in the Malay language. Understandably, Television Malaysia programs are much less popular and attract mainly members of the Malay community in Singapore. Their presence nevertheless makes them potential competitors which the RTS planners cannot ignore in program production and scheduling.

Table 6

Radio and Television Licenses, 1966–1976 (end of period)

Year	Radio Licenses	Radio and Television Licenses
1966	78,579	83,944
1967	79,277	96,164
1968	78,947	113,313
1969	80,258	130,705
1970	80,008	156,848
1971	75,586	179,178
1972	70,548	204,847
1973	69,966	230,652
1974	67,808	252,207
1975	64,211	280,479
1976	60,148	309,276

Source: Department of Statistics, 1977, p. 226.

About 50 transmission hours of education programs per week, produced and provided by the Singapore Educational Media Service (SEMS), are available on television in Singapore. These programs are prepared under the supervision of the Ministry of Education and transmitted by RTS on one channel during the daytime on weekdays. The programs are designed for primary and secondary school students.

Another type of broadcast service available in Singapore is the wire broadcasting provided by Rediffusion, a privately owned and operated company whose service dates back to 1949 and the colonial period. Rediffusion operates a commercial audio broadcasting system over cables throughout Singapore under government franchise. For a monthly rental, the company provides and installs a speaker with a selector switch and volume control at clients' premises. Since no power is required in the listener's premise, and there is no cost to the client after installation, the listener usually leaves it on for long hours everyday. Many subscriptions come from street-corner shops, restaurants, barber shops, and so on.

Programs in the Rediffusion service are broadcast over two channels, one exclusively for Chinese language programs, and the other for a combination of both Chinese and English. The combined daily transmission of the two channels amounts to 36 hours, approximately 70 percent of which are in Mandarin and several Chinese dialects, and the rest in English. As a commercial enterprise, Rediffusion presents programs that are mainly entertaining in nature, catering to a predominantly Chinese audience. News programs provided by RTS are broadcast in English, Mandarin, Hokkien, Teochew and Cantonese.

Rediffusion claimed to have a total set-count of over 86,000 in 1976 (see Table 7) and reached a total adult Chinese audience of 229,000 in 1975 (Association of Accredited Advertising Agents 1977: 90). It is understood

Table 7

Rediffusion Subscribers, 1966-1976 (end of period)

Year	Subscribers
1966	47,346
1967	48,568
1968	52,181
1969	57,034
1970	60,704
1971	63,791
1972	68,903
1973	74,689
1974	82,202
1975	85,567
1976	86,672

Source: Department of Statistics, 1977, p. 226.

that the government has been discouraging the "diffusion" of Rediffusion service in Singapore by imposing various restrictions on the laying of cables, thus limiting circuits to certain areas.

Films and Cinemas

In rather keen competition with television, cinematographic films remain a very popular form of entertainment in Singapore. Statistics show that there were 73 cinemas, 54 of them air-conditioned, in the city-republic in 1976. The total seating capacity was estimated to be 63,000 (more than 27 per 1,000 population), with a total attendance of 38,793,000 in that year (Table 8). A more recent figure reveals that total attendance increased to 43,049,178 in 1977 (*Sin Chew Jit Poh*, February 5, 1978), further indicating the growing popularity of movies as a form of entertainment among Singaporeans.

Since there is not yet a viable film industry in Singapore, practically all the feature films shown in the local cinemas are imported. According to statistics from the Ministry of Culture, Hong Kong is the republic's largest supplier of feature films; in 1976, 213 original prints of full-length films were imported from Hong Kong, excluding those sent there for subtitling. Other major suppliers were the United States (155 prints), India (115), Italy (49), the United Kingdom (48), Taiwan (43), and Indonesia (20) (H. Chong 1977, p. 31). A few feature films were also imported from France, North Korea, South Korea, Japan, Malaysia, and China.

Chinese-language films, predominantly in Mandarin, are by far the most popular, attracting about two-thirds of the total movie-goers in 1975 (Table 9). They are followed by English-language films, mostly from Hollywood. Films in Tamil and Malay languages together shared a small audience of less

Table 8

Cinemas, Seating Capacity and Attendance, 1966-1976

	Cinemas			Total Seating	
	Total	Air Conditioned	Other	Capacity	Attendance
Year	N	N	N	(000)	(000)
1966	75	32	43	57	25,910
1967	74	34	40	57	27,099
1968	75	34	41	58	28,231
1969	72	35	37	58	28,893
1970	72	36	36	55	27,980
1971	71	39	32	55	32,186
1972	74	44	30	59	36,723
1973	72	52	20	61	31,877
1974	73	52	21	62	40,068
1975	71	50	21	60	41,306
1976	73	54	19	63	38,793

Source: Department of Statistics, 1977, p. 228.

than six percent. Most of the films shown in Singapore are provided with subtitles in one or more languages. Mandarin films are usually subtitled in both Chinese and English, and many English-language films are subtitled in Chinese and Malay languages.

The majority of the cinemas in Singapore are owned by three companies—Shaw Brothers, Cathay Organization, and Chong Gay—which also produce films in Hong Kong and Taiwan and serve as distributors in Asia.

Feature films are imported into Singapore with duplicate prints. Of all Chinese films imported in 1976, the number of duplicate prints far exceeded that of the original prints (H. Chong 1977, p. 31). Most of the Chinese-language films are screened simultaneously in as many as five or six cinemas, to cater to the population in different areas of the city.

In an exploratory study by Lim, Liu-Tan and Foo (1975), a sample of films (N = 318) screened in Singapore cinemas from October 1974 to March 1975 were analyzed according to source, content and theme, with the following findings: (1) About 84 percent of films screened in Singapore during the six-month period were imported from Asia. (2) Among the films from Asia, 39.4 percent were categorized as "sex, violence, and horror" and 35.6 percent were drama. (3) Of the films from outside Asia, "sex, violence, and horror" predominated in 68.8 percent. Thus "sex, violence, and horror" films account for a very high proportion of those imported and screened in Singapore.

All cinematographic films intended for public exhibition, sale, or circulation in Singapore are subject to previewing and censorship by the Board of Film Censors within the Ministry of Culture. The Board is also responsible for inspection of all film accessories and publicity materials. For a discussion of the policy of the Board of Film Censors, see chapter 5.

Table 9

Cinema Attendance by Language of Film, 1975–1976

Language* of Film	Estimated Attendance per Week	Percentage
English	250,200	28.6
Chinese	574,900	65.7
Malay	21,500	2.4
Indian	29,000	3.3
Total	875,600	100.0

Source: Computation and estimation based on Association of Accredited Advertising Agents, 1977, p. 94–99.

*Each category includes languages or dialects from the same broad language group.

Telecommunication

As Singapore is expanding its role as a global city, striving to become an international trade center, a financial and banking center and a servicing center, the availability of international telecommunication services within the infrastructure is essential. The development of a comprehensive telecommunication system, including telephone, telex, telegraph, and satellite communication facilities, has been given high priority. Growth and expansion of telecommunications in Singapore have been phenomenal.

To facilitate the development and operation of telecommunication facilities, the Telecommunication Authority of Singapore (Telecom) was incorporated by an act of parliament in 1974, with authority to provide and operate both national and international services. It is the licensing authority and adviser to the government for all telecommunication operations.

The strategic position of Singapore on world trade routes makes it the focus of sea and air transportation as well as a center for commercial, banking, financial, and shipping services. Consequently, its telecommunications service is very internationally oriented.

International telephone service to and from Singapore (either person-to-person or station-to-station) was available to 184 countries in the world as of April 1978. In January 1976, fully automatic International Direct Dialing (IDD) was introduced and by February 1978 was available to 21 countries, and to be extended from 21 to 41 countries by 1978–1979 (*Sunday Times,* February 12, 1978).

As of February 1978, international data transmission and switched telephone service known as "datel service" was available to Australia, Canada, Denmark, France, Hong Kong, New Zealand, Britain, and the United States (*Sunday Times,* February 12, 1978).

With the commissioning of the automatic computer-based International

Telex Exchange in July 1974, telex services became computer-switched, and subscribers can obtain direct telex connections overseas if the country of destination possesses automatic receiving facilities. As of April 1977, Telecom provided international telex service to 165 countries with automatic keying to 100 countries.

The three major international services (telex, telegraph, and telephone) are provided on a 24-hour basis in Singapore in collaboration with international and regional organizations like the International Telecommunication Union (ITU), Commonwealth Telecommunication Organization (CTO), and the International Telecommunication Satellite Organization (Intelsat). In 1975, Singapore ranked 17th of the 93 member nations of Intelsat in terms of the volume of use of satellite telecommunication. International telex and telephone calls have yearly growth rates of 44.5 percent and 28.2 percent respectively. There has been a decline in the use of telegrams in recent years (see Table 10), but from 1966 to 1976, the number of telex subscribers increased from 159 to 2,240, or approximately one telex machine per 1,000 population (*Straits Times*, October 4, 1977).

The rapid growth in the demand for external telecommunication services, according to a member of parliament (MP) and local economist, Dr. Ow Chin Hock, can be attributed to "the change of Singapore's industrial strategy, its export promotion, the inflow of foreign investment particularly from multinational corporations and its development into a major financial and service sector" (*Straits Times,* October 4, 1977).

Singapore's important role in world communication is reflected in its status as the western terminus of the Commonwealth Telephone Cable

Table 10

Frequency of Telegrams, Telex Calls, and International Telephone Calls, 1966–1976 (in thousands)

	Outgoing Telegrams		Outgoing Telex Calls		International
Year	Peninsular Malaysia	Other Countries	Peninsular Malaysia	Other Countries	Telephone Calls*
1966	436	607	18	29	75
1967	421	705	24	38	105
1968	361	750	30	47	141
1969	357	798	31	66	182
1970	176	910	33	103	255
1971	96	972	28	176	350
1972	86	1,015	37	319	431
1973	76	1,140	44	528	577
1974	74	1,039	61	914	707
1975	68	840	110	1,552	843
1976	55	798	176	2,154	1,077

Source: Department of Statistics, 1977, p. 135.

*Figures exclude calls to Peninsular Malaysia.

System, which crosses Southeast Asia to Australia (SEACOM), the Pacific from Australia to Canada (COMPAC), and the Atlantic to Britain (CANTAT). Singapore is also a major international relay center for air and sea communications and for meteorological information on behalf of the World Meteorological Organization (WMO).

Space communication in Singapore began with the operation of the Sentosa Communication Satellite Earth Station in August 1971. The first antenna beams toward the Intelsat IV satellite positioned 35,800 km above the Indian Ocean, enabling Singapore to communicate directly with 14 countries, namely Britain, Bangladesh, Greece, Germany, Hong Kong, Israel, Italy, Indonesia, India, Japan, the Philippines, Sri Lanka, Thailand, and Taiwan. The second antenna, commissioned in August 1974, works with the Intelsat IV satellite positioned above the Pacific Ocean, enabling Singapore to communicate directly with Australia, Canada, South Korea, New Zealand, Mainland China, and the United States.

Telecom plans to reconfigure the existing earth station in preparation for the future system implementation plans of the International Telecommunication Satellite Organization for the Intelsat IV-A Series (1978-1989) and the next generation of satellites known as the Intelsat V Series (1980-1982). It is also planning to study the provision of another earth station.

The Maritime Satellite (Marisat) service was introduced in Singapore for telephone service in February 1971; for telex service in April 1977; and for telegraph service in November 1977. It supplements international high frequency radio maritime services and enables high quality communications between ships in international waters and Singapore users, via the US Marisat system. Telecom is also planning to take part in the International Maritime Satellite Organization (Inmarsat) to establish a maritime satellite system for the use of world shipping in the 1980s.

Singapore's international services are supported by an efficient domestic telephone network. As of February 1978, there were 327,000 telephone lines and 460,000 telephones installed in Singapore. With about 20 telephones for every 100 people, Singapore ranks third in East Asia in terms of telephone density, next to Japan and Hong Kong (*Straits Times,* February 15, 1978). This facility is complemented by 1,602 public phones and 3,012 coin-operated telephones in the republic (*The Mirror,* March 13, 1978).

Radio paging service has been available since October 1973. Mobile radio telephones are also offered by Telecom to provide landmobile service for motor vehicles and harbor craft. In April 1977, the Automatic Mobile Telephone Service was introduced to provide an automatic network with push-button dialing for the landmobile subscribers (*Straits Times,* February 2, 1978).

Due to improvement in the standard of living and rapid expansion of public housing units, the domestic demand for telephone services in Singapore is growing very rapidly. In early 1978, new applicants for telephones averaged 6,000 per month. At the same time, requests for telephone removals have also increased, averaging 1,700 per month in early 1978 (*Straits*

Times, February 4, 1978). As a result, telecom has not been able to provide immediate service upon request for phone installment. Such delay in service has been the main source of complaints against Telecom for years, for many applicants may have to wait several months until a line is available. One of Telecom's priority objectives is to reduce the number of such deferred subscribers and their waiting time. In early 1978, the total number of deferred subscribers had been reduced from 30,000 in March 1976 to 2,650 at the end of 1977 (*Straits Times*, February 4, 1978). Up to 90 percent of new applicants are now provided with immediate service (*Straits Times*, February 15, 1978).

Postal Services

Postal services in Singapore are provided by the Postal Services Department under the jurisdiction and control of the Ministry of Communication. According to the Postmaster-General, Mr. Wong Lee Hoong, in 1977 there were a total of 62 post offices supplemented by two mobile post offices, 49 postal agencies, 190 licensed stamp vendors and 448 posting boxes. An average of 520,000 postal articles were collected daily in Singapore. Of these, about 75 percent were delivered locally, and the rest were for overseas mailing. In 1977, of 460 persons employed for the delivery of mails, 30 percent were motorized. Others used either bicycle or foot. On the average, each delivered 1,000 postal items per day (*Sin Chew Jit Poh*, July 28, 1977). The amount of mail handled has been increasing rapidly, with an annual growth rate of about five percent since 1960. In 1976, a total of 350 million postal articles were handled by the Postal Services Department (see Table 11). Of these, some 149 million articles were posted in Singapore (*The Mirror*, October 17, 1977).

In 1977, the Postal Department introduced the Local Urgent Mail Service to transmit urgent correspondence and documents from one point of Singapore to another. The service covers both collection and delivery of urgent mails. An urgent mail item posted under this service (at any of 20 selected post offices) will be delivered within two and a half hours of its collection at special scheduled collection times (*Straits Times*, June 23, 1977).

The functions of postal services in Singapore include more than just collection and delivery of mails. Through arrangement with various government agencies, the post offices also provide the following general services: collection of Central Provident Fund contributions, payment of public assistance allowances and pensions, issue and renewal of radio-television licenses, renewal of driving licenses and the sale of area licenses. The Postal Department also makes use of postmarks to publicize its own work, to inform the public of its service, and, most important, to help publicize national campaigns being promoted in the republic.

Table 11

Frequency and Types of Postal Articles Handled, 1966–1976 (in thousands)

Year	Total	Letters	Post-cards	Printed Matter	Airmail Corres-pondence First Class	Registered Articles	Parcels	Unregistered Government Franked Corres-pondence	Other
1966	170,252	48,903	1,040	68,176	23,493	5,206	1,468	21,958	8
1967	192,555	51,558	1,581	66,732	41,435	5,796	1,745	23,699	9
1968	197,634	54,658	1,216	71,843	36,464	6,645	1,523	25,277	8
1969	219,009	55,857	1,514	86,231	37,208	6,921	1,657	29,614	7
1970	239,058	56,198	2,026	100,372	42,153	7,061	1,757	29,480	11
1971	268,094	70,322	1,742	118,780	43,331	8,188	1,766	23,945	20
1972	282,824	81,722	1,794	123,521	46,633	8,122	1,759	19,258	15
1973	299,148	144,895	2,616	65,447	57,723	8,148	1,804	18,498	17
1974	315,142	144,618	2,547	73,568	58,647	9,397	1,711	24,636	18
1975	331,447	158,352	1,772	72,432	59,761	10,514	1,650	26,953	13
1976	350,172	161,404	2,359	82,211	59,845	11,195	1,664	31,483	11

Source: Department of Statistics, 1977, p. 134.

4

Media Habits and Information Needs: An Audience Analysis

Until recently, there has been an acute lack of information on media behavior and information needs of the audience in Singapore. In 1977, a survey[2] was conducted by the authors under the sponsorship of the Asian Mass Communication Research and Information Center (AMIC) in an attempt to identify the patterns of media habits among Singaporeans and to find out the kinds of information needed by the audience. Such information is essential for communication planning per se and social development planning in general.

In this chapter the results of the media survey are used to analyze audience behavior and perceptions toward four major types of mass media: newspapers, radio, television, and cinema. A comparison is made to indicate relative functionality and status among various channels of information in fulfilling the needs of the audience.

Newspapers

The Changing Newspaper Readership

As we have pointed out in chapter 3, up to 1976, Chinese language dailies have been the most widely circulated among all language newspapers. However, this pattern is changing: there has been a noticeable decline in recent years in the readership of Chinese newspapers giving place to English language newspapers. Because of the increasingly dominant status of English and the emphasis on bilingualism in Singapore, both the circulation and the percentage of readership of the English-language newspapers will soon exceed those of the Chinese newspapers. This seems to justify recent speculation that a fourth English newspaper may be set up by the owner of a major Chinese newspaper in the near future. If this happens, the

[2]The survey is based on a quota sample of 612 Singaporeans aged 15 and over. The factors stratified in sampling are sex, ethnicity, working status and housing type. The detailed findings of the study are reported in Chen and Kuo (1978).

English press will undoubtedly enjoy the majority of the newspaper readership in Singapore.

The newspaper circulation rate in 1976 was 209 papers per 1,000 population. But circulation figures do not necessarily reflect the amount of readership, because each copy of a newspaper may be shared by a larger or smaller number of readers and an individual may read more than one daily newspaper. The results of the survey show that 29.3 percent of the respondents subscribe to two newspapers, and 6.4 percent to three or more newspapers. In terms of home subscriptions, the four largest newspapers are: *Straits Times* (60.4%), *Sin Chew Jit Poh* (26.6%), *Nanyang Siang Pau* (18.7%) and *New Nation* (11.8%). But, the order changes for readership: *Straits Times* is still the largest (68.5%); *New Nation* is second largest (47.3%); and *Sin Chew Jit Poh* (30.0%) and *Nanyang Siang Pau* (23.6%) drop to third and fourth respectively. Thus, although *New Nation* has the smallest home subscription rate of the four newspapers, it attracts a large readership.

More than 80 percent of the respondents read newspapers daily. Among them, 60.2 percent spend one hour or more reading newspapers every day. More males (91.8%) than females (68.8%) read newspapers daily, and males usually spend more time than females reading newspapers. For example, 69.2 percent of male readers spend one hour or more every day, compared to only 49.4 percent of females who spend the same amount of time.

Views on Newspaper Contents

When reading a newspaper, people usually read the international news section first (44.5%), followed by national and local news sections (28.1%),

Table 12

Section in the Newspaper That Respondents Usually Read First, by Sex (percent)

Section	Male	Female	Both
International news	49.4	38.5	44.5
National/local news	20.5	37.5	28.1
Crime/sensational	6.0	15.5	10.2
Sports	19.3	1.0	11.1
Editorial	0.8	0.0	0.4
Letters to the editor	0.8	1.0	0.9
Other (business, education, etc.)	3.2	6.5	4.8
Total* Percent	100.0	100.0	100.0
Number	249	200	449

*Newspaper readers, not including those who rarely or never read newspapers.

sports (11.1%), and crime and sensational news (10.2%). Very few people will first read the following sections: editorial, letters to the editor, cartoons, advertisements, and religious and cultural sections (Table 12). Apart from international and local news, which the majority of both males and females read first, more males (19.3%) than females (1.0%) read the sports section. But more females (15.5%) than males (6.0%) read crime and sensational news. A comparison of reading habits among various age groups show that younger people read sports news, and more older people read crime and sensational news.

Table 13 shows that the five most popular sections in the newspapers in Singapore are, in order: national and local news, international news, crime and sensational news, sports, and letters to the editor. The five least popular sections are business, religious reports, serialized stories, women's section, and editorials. As shown in Table 14, the sections in the newspaper which are considered to be very important are national and local news (69.2%), international news (54.0%), crime and sensational news (39.8%), sports (27.4%), and letters to the editor (27.0%).

Regarding the adequacy of the contents of various sections in the newspapers, more than 70 percent of the readers in the survey consider the contents of advertisements and national and local news adequate. More than 60 percent consider those of crime and sensational news and international news adequate. A total of 53.6 percent consider the coverage of sports adequate. More than 40 percent consider the contents of letters to the editor, cartoons, serialized stories, and editorials adequate (Table 15).

Table 13

How Much Respondents Like the Various Sections in the Newspapers (percent)

Section	Very Much	Some	Do Not Like	Total Readers* %	Total Readers* N
International news	40.4	42.4	17.4	100.0	540
National/local news	57.5	34.0	8.5	100.0	544
Business	8.4	23.8	67.8	100.0	534
Crime/sensational	38.9	48.7	12.4	100.0	540
Sports	34.0	34.9	31.1	100.0	538
Cultural/educational	19.7	38.2	42.1	100.0	542
Religious	13.2	22.7	64.1	100.0	537
Editorial	16.7	38.8	44.5	100.0	534
Letters to the editor	27.5	39.5	33.0	100.0	539
Women's	20.7	32.5	46.8	100.0	542
Juvenile/youth	16.4	41.8	41.8	100.0	538
Cartoons	26.7	29.1	44.2	100.0	539
Serialized stories	19.6	32.4	48.0	100.0	540
Advertisements	16.3	47.9	35.8	100.0	541

*Newspaper readers.

Table 14

Importance of Various Sections in the Newspapers (percent)

Section	Very Much	Some	Not Important	Total Readers* %	N
International news	54.0	35.4	10.6	100.0	545
National/local news	69.2	26.0	4.8	100.0	546
Business	12.5	31.1	56.4	100.0	544
Crime/sensational	39.8	49.4	10.8	100.0	545
Sports	27.4	42.3	30.3	100.0	544
Cultural/educational	25.9	39.3	34.8	100.0	545
Religious	15.7	23.8	60.5	100.0	543
Editorial	21.8	39.6	38.6	100.0	541
Letters to the editor	27.0	44.8	28.2	100.0	545
Women's	15.1	37.2	47.7	100.0	543
Juvenile/youth	19.9	42.3	37.8	100.0	542
Cartoons	16.5	29.8	53.7	100.0	545
Serialized stories	13.2	35.2	51.6	100.0	545
Advertisements	18.5	47.5	34.0	100.0	547

*Newspaper readers.

Table 15

Adequacy of Contents of Various Sections in the Newspapers (percent)

Section	Adequate	Inadequate	Cannot Say	Total Readers* %	N
International news	61.7	15.0	23.3	100.0	546
National/local news	70.8	13.5	15.7	100.0	541
Business	31.1	5.6	63.3	100.0	540
Crime/sensational	63.7	13.3	23.0	100.0	540
Sports	53.6	15.0	31.4	100.0	539
Cultural/educational	32.2	22.8	45.0	100.0	540
Religious	16.5	24.3	59.2	100.0	540
Editorial	41.5	11.1	47.4	100.0	540
Letters to the editor	43.0	19.7	37.3	100.0	539
Women's	35.6	16.9	47.5	100.0	540
Juvenile/youth	34.0	18.0	48.0	100.0	538
Cartoons	42.3	17.3	40.4	100.0	539
Serialized stories	42.3	13.4	44.3	100.0	537
Advertisements	70.9	3.7	25.4	100.0	539

*Newspaper readers.

Radio

Radio Audience

Compared to newspaper and television, radio is a less popular and less important medium in Singapore. Results of our survey show that only 44.3 percent of the respondents listen to radio daily, 19.6 percent several times a week, 6.9 percent once a week or less, and 29.2 percent rarely or never listen to radio (Table 16).

More females than males listen to radio, and spend more time doing so. Table 16 shows that 48.0 percent of females listen to radio daily, but only 40.5 percent of males do so; 37.0 percent of females spend more than one hour a day listening to radio compared to 24.1 percent of males.

Among the three major ethnic groups, 70.4 percent of Malays listen to radio daily; Indians are second with 53.2 percent; followed by Chinese with 37.3 percent. Only 5.1 percent of Malays and 8.5 percent of Indians have rarely or never listened to radio, compared with 37.3 percent of the Chinese. Malays and Indians spend more time listening to radio than do Chinese.

Views on Radio Programs

The four most popular radio programs are pop and light music (44.7%), news and current affairs (21.8%), drama and short stories (15.6%), and sports (6.4%). As with TV programs, radio programs on youth and children (0.9%), science (1.2%), and women (2.3%) are not popular (Table 17). Pop

Table 16

Listening to Radio by Sex
(percent)

		Male	Female	Both
How Often				
Daily		40.5	48.0	44.3
Several times a week		27.8	11.5	19.6
Once a week or less		6.2	7.5	6.9
Rarely or never		25.5	33.0	29.2
Total*	Percent	100.0	100.0	100.0
	Number	306	306	612
How Much Time				
< ½ hour		24.1	13.2	18.9
½-1 hour		51.8	49.8	50.9
1-3 hours		16.7	21.0	18.7
> 3 hours		7.4	16.0	11.5
Total*	Percent	100.0	100.0	100.0
	Number	228	205	433

*Radio audience, not including those who rarely or never listen to radio.

Table 17

Preferred Types of Radio Programs, by Sex (percent)

Program		Male	Female	Both
News/current affairs		27.7	15.1	21.8
Sports		11.7	0.5	6.4
Science		1.3	1.0	1.2
Women's		0.0	4.9	2.3
Youth/children's		1.3	0.5	0.9
Pop and light music		45.5	43.9	44.7
Classical and serious music		4.8	4.4	4.6
Drama and short stories		6.1	26.3	15.6
Other		1.6	3.4	2.5
Total*	Percent	100.0	100.0	100.0
	Number	230	205	435

*Radio audience.

music and news are popular programs with both males and females. Sports programs are much more popular with males while drama and short stories are better liked by females.

Favorite radio programs vary among different age groups. Younger people (15–34 years of age) tend to like pop music and sports, and older age groups (over 35 years) like news, drama and short stories, and classical and serious music.

Generally speaking, the amount of time allotted to each type of radio program is considered adequate by the respondents, probably because they do not care much about them anyway. The four programs which are considered most adequate are: news and current affairs (66.5%), pop and light music (65.7%), drama and short stories (48.6%), and sports (40.9%). These four types of programs are also the most popular (Table 18).

Television

Television Audience

Television is a very popular medium in Singapore. According to the 1972 ESCAP survey (P. Chen 1973), 76.4 percent of the respondents claimed to have watched television. This figure increased to 90.3 percent in our 1977 survey, which showed that 64.1 percent of respondents watch television daily, 21.8 percent several times a week, and 4.4 percent once a week or less. Only 9.7 percent rarely or never watch television (Table 19).

Between the two sexes, more females watch television and for longer periods of time. As many as 68.2 percent of females and 60.1 percent of males watch television daily. More than 20 percent of females spend more than three hours watching television every day, compared to 16.7 percent of males (Table 19). Younger age groups do not watch television as regularly as the

Table 18

Adequacy of Time Allotted to Various Radio Programs (percent)

Program	Adequate	Inadequate	Cannot Say	Total* %	Total* N
News/current affairs	66.5	11.2	22.3	100.0	436
Sports	40.9	9.5	49.6	100.0	433
Science	21.5	13.2	65.3	100.0	432
Women's	30.6	11.4	58.0	100.0	431
Youth/children's	35.4	8.3	56.3	100.0	432
Pop and light music	65.7	16.7	17.6	100.0	432
Classical and serious music	30.9	9.5	59.6	100.0	431
Drama and short stories	48.6	10.4	41.0	100.0	432
Others (religion, arts, etc.)	22.3	17.4	60.3	100.0	430

*Radio audience.

Table 19

Television Watching by Sex (percent)

		Male	Female	Both
How Often				
Daily		60.1	68.2	64.1
Several times a week		26.8	16.7	21.8
Once a week or less		4.2	4.6	4.4
Rarely or never		8.9	10.5	9.7
Total*	Percent	100.0	100.0	100.0
	Number	306	305	611
How Much Time				
< ½ hour		36.3	29.0	32.7
1–2 hours		32.7	33.5	33.1
2–3 hours		14.3	16.9	15.6
>3 hours		16.7	20.6	18.6
Total*	Percent	100.0	100.0	100.0
	Number	281	272	553

*TV audience, not including those who rarely or never watch TV.

older group does, but on the average they spend more time watching it every day. For example, 68.4 percent of those aged 45 years or older watch television daily, but only 59.8 percent of those between 15 and 24 years do so. However, 23 percent of this younger group spends more than three hours daily watching television, compared with only 12.9 percent of the 45-plus age-group.

Of the three major ethnic groups in Singapore, 76.5 percent of the Malays watch television daily, compared to 61.9 percent of the Chinese and 55.3 percent of the Indians. While 28.4 percent of the Malays spend more than three hours watching television every day, only 15.4 percent of the Chinese and 21.7 percent of the Indians spend as much.

Views on TV Programs

The most popular TV programs are movies and TV series, which more than 50 percent of the TV audience in the sample indicated that they like most (Table 20); less popular TV programs are forums and topics of the week (0.9%), youth and juvenile programs (0.6%), women's programs (1.1%) and educational and science programs (2.5%). Movies and TV series (60.4%) and news and current affairs (17.2%) are the two most popular TV programs for women, whereas for men the most popular are movies and TV series (42.1%), sports (20.1%), and news and current affairs (20.1%). When respondents were asked to indicate the types of TV programs most important to them, the majority mentioned news and current affairs (50.0%) instead. This is especially true of the male audience, 56.1 percent of whom stated that news and current affairs are the most important TV programs to them, compared to only 43.5 percent of the female respondents.

Table 20

Types of TV Programs That Respondents Like Most, by Sex (percent)

Program		Male	Female	Both
News/current affairs		20.1	17.2	18.7
Forum/topic of the week		0.7	1.1	0.9
Sports		20.1	0.7	10.5
Education/science		2.9	2.2	2.5
Movie/drama/TV serials		42.1	60.4	51.2
Variety shows		12.2	14.3	13.2
Juvenile/youth		0.7	0.4	0.6
Women's		0.0	2.2	1.1
Other (serious music, religion, etc.)		1.2	1.5	1.3
Total*	Percent	100.0	100.0	100.0
	Number	277	273	550

*TV audience.

Different age groups expressed a variety of views on their favorite TV programs. The older group (45 years and over) prefer movies and TV series (61.4%) and news and current affairs (25.7%). For the younger audience (15–24 years old), the favorite programs are movies and TV series (48.6%), variety shows (18.0%), sports (14.9%), and news and current affairs (12.9%). Different ethnic groups also have their different preferences. The Chinese audience prefers movies and TV series (54.3%) and variety shows (14.7%). Malays and Indians favor movies and TV series (40.6% and 47.8% respectively), and news and current affairs (27.1% and 30.4% respectively). All ethnic groups and age groups have, however, similar views on the types of programs that are most important to them. News and current affairs (50.0%) and movies and TV series (26.6%) are considered by all to be the two most important.

Regarding the adequacy of the amount of time allotted to various TV programs, the results of the survey show that movies and TV serials, news and current affairs, and variety shows are perceived to be adequate by 72.6 percent, 70.0 percent, and 56.7 percent respectively (Table 21). When this finding is compared with that of the respondents' favorite TV programs as discussed in the preceding paragraphs, it is obvious that those thought to have adequate amount of coverage are also the most popular ones.

Language Medium and TV Channels

Television programs are transmitted in all four official languages and several Chinese dialects, mainly Cantonese and Hokkien. There is a very high correlation between the ethnic background of the audience and the

Table 21

Adequacy of Time Allotted to Various Programs (percent)

Program	Adequate	Inadequate	Cannot Say	Total* %	Total* N
News/current affairs	70.0	9.1	20.9	100.0	550
Forum/topic of the week	28.0	14.1	57.9	100.0	546
Sports	48.5	18.1	33.4	100.0	546
Education/science	33.6	18.3	48.1	100.0	547
Movies/drama/TV serials	72.6	17.0	10.4	100.0	548
Variety shows	56.7	25.1	18.2	100.0	545
Juvenile/youth	29.1	17.9	53.0	100.0	543
Women's	29.3	14.3	56.4	100.0	546
Others (serious music,religion, etc.)	17.8	17.7	64.5	100.0	538

*TV audience.

language of TV programs watched. TV programs in the Malay and Tamil languages are most popular among members of the Malay and Indian communities respectively. Although Chinese programs are also most popular among the Chinese audience, they attract some audience from other ethnic communities. For example, 26.3 percent of the Malay and 23.9 percent of the Indian audience indicated that they often watch Chinese programs. Subtitles make it possible for various ethnic groups to watch TV programs in other languages. English language programs are, however, shared by audiences from all three major ethnic communities. We find 97.9 percent of the Malay, 93.5 percent of the Indian, and 84.0 percent of the Chinese audiences often watch TV programs in English. In general, younger people are more interested in watching English TV programs than older people. For instance, 94.8 percent of the 15-24 age group indicated that they often watch English TV programs, compared to 79.7 percent of the older population (45 years and over). The majority of the respondents (75.9%) find that subtitles are very useful to them. Only 10.9 percent stated that subtitles are not useful. The remaining 13.2 percent stated that it depends on the circumstances.

Television audiences in Singapore can receive both channels (5 and 8) of Television Singapore and two channels (3 and 10) of Television Malaysia. The latter channels provide only black and white programs, mostly in the Malay language. Findings of the survey show that the two Television Malaysia channels are much less popular and attract mainly members of the Malay and Indian communities. Only 5.1 percent of the audience stated that they most like Channels 3 and 10 (Television Malaysia), compared to 50.6 percent for Channel 5 and 44.3 percent for Channel 8 (Television Singapore).

Children and Television

In many Singapore families, children decide on the selection of TV programs. In our survey, 36.8 percent of the audience indicated that children usually select the program; 12.5 percent indicated that the father of the family makes the decision, and only 4.8 percent indicated that the mother makes the decision. In most cases (45.9%) none of the above can be identified as the main decision-maker. Among the Malays, as many as 51.6 percent indicated that children usually select the TV programs (Table 22).

Children in Singapore spend an average of 80 minutes watching TV programs daily. Twenty-six percent of the children spend more than two hours, 34 percent spend one to two hours, and 40 percent spend less than one hour.

The majority of the parents among the audience (62.8%) consider that the amount of time their children spend watching television is just about right, while 23.1 percent of them consider their children spend too much time watching television. The remaining 14.1 percent have no opinion. Two-fifths of the parents stated that they do not have any control over the type of TV programs their children watch, while 40.6 percent have some control and only 19.4 percent have much control.

Cinema

At the time of our survey, there were 73 cinemas in the republic, with a total annual attendance of 38,793,000 in 1976. The average weekly attendance is 746,019; that is, about one-third of the total population attends cinema shows once a week.

According to the survey, 90.3 percent of the respondents have been to the movies at least once. In terms of frequency, 24.1 percent of the movie-goers go to the movies about once a week, 35.1 percent once or twice a month, 21.6 percent several times a year, 9.5 percent rarely go to movies, and 9.7 percent never do so. The younger people (15–34 years old) attend cinema shows more often than the older group (35 years and over). For example, more than 30 percent of the younger movie-goers, but less than 10 percent of the older group, go to movies about once a week.

When people go to the movies, most of them go with companions. Age (and thus marital status) appears to have much to do with the type of companions people go with. For instance, 75.6 percent of the younger movie-goers (15-24 years of age) but only 6.1 percent of the older people (35-44 years of age), go to the movies with friends and colleagues. On the other hand, 88.2 percent of the older people, but only 17.2 percent of the younger group, go to the movies with family members. In terms of educational background, the Chinese-educated (62.2%) usually go to the movies with family members, but the English-educated (52.2%) are more likely to go with friends and colleagues.

In general, Chinese, Malay, and Indian films attract audiences mainly from their own ethnic groups. The English-language films, however, attract audiences from all ethnic groups. As shown in Table 23, 76.5 percent of the movie-goers in the sample often or sometimes go to English films. The

Table 22

Who Decides on Selecting TV Programs by Ethnic Group (percent)

	Chinese	Malay	Indian*	Others	All Ethnic Groups
Father	12.0	14.7	10.9	14.2	12.5
Mother	4.5	3.2	10.9	4.8	4.8
Children	33.5	51.6	26.1	52.4	36.8
No single one of the above	50.0	30.5	52.1	28.6	45.9
Total Percent	100.0	100.0	100.0	100.0	100.0
Number†	382	95	46	21	544

*Indian is an official census category used in Singapore to refer to people of South Asian (India, Pakistan, Bangladesh, and Sri Lanka) origin.
†TV audience.

Table 23

Languages/Dialects of Movies Attended,* by Ethnic Group (percent)

Language	Chinese	Malay	Indian†	Others	All Ethnic Groups
English	74.8	85.0	85.0	94.7	76.5
Malay	1.7	72.5	7.5	0.0	12.5
Tamil	1.2	9.0	77.5	5.3	8.1
Mandarin	93.1	19.2	7.7	20.0	73.8

*Often or sometimes.

†Indian is an official census category used in Singapore to refer to people of South Asian (India, Pakistan, Bangladesh, and Sri Lanka) origin.

percentages are 73.8 percent for Chinese films, 12.5 percent for Malay films, and 8.1 percent for Indian films. The figures reflect that a great number of the population have seen films in more than one language. However, English-language films and Chinese-language films are the most popular. Thus 91.3 percent of those between 15 and 24 years of age go to English films, but only 48.3 percent of those aged 45 years or over do so (Table 24).

The most popular types of movies are drama and romance (31.7%), crime and violence (17.5%), thriller and mystery (15.5%), and comedy (15.2%). For female movie-goers, drama and romance (45.5%) and comedy (14.3%) are the most popular, whereas male movie-goers prefer crime and violence (22.9%) and thriller and mystery (19.3%).

Comparing Mass Media

Mass Media Exposure

The above analysis of the mass media and communication patterns in Singapore shows that the population as a whole experiences a very high level of media exposure (Table 25). Of the four major types of mass media,

Table 24

Languages/Dialects of Movies Attended,* by Age Group (percent)

Language	15-24	25-34	35-44	45 & Over	All Age Groups
English	91.3	75.0	64.5	48.3	76.5
Malay	13.1	8.1	14.3	18.6	12.5
Tamil	5.8	9.7	7.7	11.9	8.1
Mandarin	74.5	78.4	67.7	66.7	73.8

*Often or sometimes.

television is the most popular. It is interesting to note that although 92.8 percent of the respondents own radios at home, only 70.8 percent listen to them. This is possible because a radio may be attached to a stereo set, an electric clock, or a motor vehicle, and the person who owns it may never use it at all. Moreover, a family may own one or more radio sets and some members of the family may never listen to the radio.

In all major types of mass media in Singapore, all four official languages are used to make their contents available to the linguistically diversified population. However, as English is the *de facto* dominant working language in Singapore and the Chinese constitute the majority (76%) of the population, English and Chinese are the major languages used in most of the mass media. Moreover, most TV programs and all feature films are imported, mainly from the United States, Hong Kong and Taiwan, and are mostly in either English or Chinese. On the average, about 70 percent of television transmission hours are in English and Chinese. English and Chinese newspapers account for 92.7 percent of the total. Films in English and Chinese constitute 92.1 percent of all movies shown in Singapore. However, the distribution of radio transmission hours among the four official languages is quite even, since four separate language channels operate simultaneously.

The uneven distribution of the four official languages in the mass media is reduced by the use of subtitles in movies and TV programs, and by the bilingual section in most major newspapers. This is a response to the official policy of multilingualism as well as to the needs of the population.

Singaporeans seldom watch television alone; 91.0 percent of the TV

Table 25

Availability and Use of Mass Media by Ethnic Group (percent)

	Chinese	Malay	Indian*	Others	All Ethnic Groups
Media Available at Home					
Newspaper†	88.0	70.4	89.4	87.0	85.2
Television	91.2	92.9	95.7	95.7	92.0
Radio	80.7	99.0	95.7	100.0	92.8
Magazine	26.5	25.5	48.9	34.8	28.4
Use Of Media					
Read newspaper‡	89.5	86.7	95.7	87.0	89.5
Watch TV‡	88.4	96.9	95.7	91.3	90.3
Listen to radio‡	62.7	94.9	91.5	82.6	70.8
Read magazine‡	52.4	74.5	78.7	60.9	58.3
Go to movie§	93.2	80.6	85.1	87.0	90.3

*Indian is an official census category used in Singapore to refer to people of South Asian (India, Pakistan, Bangladesh, and Sri Lanka) origin.

†Subscription.

‡Using the given medium more than "rarely or never."

§Having ever gone to a movie.

audience watches television together with family members, 2.3 percent with friends and colleagues, 1.3 percent with other people, and only 5.4 percent alone. In contrast, 43.3 percent of the audience in the sample listen to radio alone, 52.2 percent with family members, 3.9 percent with friends and colleagues, and 0.6 percent with other people. When they go to the movies, 51.3 percent go with family members, 39.9 percent with friends and colleagues, 2.6 percent with other people, and only 6.2 percent alone.

Media for Urgent and Important News

People usually turn to the radio for news they want to know urgently, but turn to the newspaper for important news. To seek information on urgent news, 40.7 percent of respondents indicate that they turn to radio first, 34.1 percent choose newspaper, and 24.9 percent turn to television. But, when people want to know about important news, the majority (52.5%) choose the newspaper, 27.2 percent turn to television, and 19.8 percent turn to radio (Table 26).

It is interesting to note that more females than males turn to television for both urgent and important news, but more males turn to radio for urgent news and to newspaper for important news (Table 26). Different age groups also have different preferences for the channel of communication for urgent and important news. More younger people (15–24 years old) turn to radio for urgent news, but more older people (45 years and over) turn to television. Among the major ethnic groups, more Malays and Indians turn to radio for urgent and important news, but more Chinese turn to television for urgent and important news.

The Usefulness and Reliability of the Mass Media

Respondents were asked to evaluate the usefulness and reliability of the mass media for information on government policies and public affairs, international and current events, health and nutrition, sports, education, enter-

Table 26

Type of Medium That Respondents Turn to for Urgent and Important News, by Sex (percent)

Medium	Urgent News			Important News		
	Male	Female	Both	Male	Female	Both
Newspapers	35.1	33.0	34.1	57.0	48.0	52.5
Television	20.3	29.6	24.9	21.1	33.4	27.2
Radio	44.0	37.4	40.7	20.9	18.6	19.8
Movies and Magazines	0.6	0.0	0.3	1.0	0.0	0.5
Total Percent	100.0	100.0	100.0	100.0	100.0	100.0
Number	302	297	599	302	297	599

Table 27

Most Useful and Most Reliable Source of Information (percent)

Medium	Most Useful	Most Reliable
Newspapers	51.1	48.8
Radio	5.8	5.9
Television	22.9	25.7
Movies	3.1	2.5
Magazines	7.9	8.2
Personal Sources	9.2	8.9
Total Percent	100.0	100.0
Number	612	612

tainment, and business and jobs. Generally, newspapers are rated by the majority of the respondents (51.1%) as the most useful source for various types of information. This is followed by television (22.9%), personal sources[3] (9.2%), magazines (7.9%), and movies (3.1%) (Table 27).

As shown in Table 28, newspapers are most useful for almost all types of information, except entertainment, for which television is the most useful. Television is a useful source for entertainment and sports. Movies are not important as a source of information, but are important for entertainment. Magazines are a useful source of information on health and nutrition, and education. Personal sources are useful for health and nutrition, and business and job information.

For information on government policies and public affairs, 67.8 percent

Table 28

Respondents Who Believe the Various Media to Be the Most Useful Source, by Type of Information (percent)

Types of Information	News-paper	Radio	TV	Movie	Magazine	Personal Source	Total %	Total N
Govt. Policies/ Public Affairs	67.8	8.0	17.4	0.2	1.4	5.2	100.0	596
International/ Current Events	63.2	6.4	19.9	0.0	7.4	3.1	100.0	582
Health/Nutrition	27.7	9.4	16.5	0.2	23.4	22.9	100.0	577
Sports	47.1	5.2	39.4	0.6	4.4	3.3	100.0	570
Education	45.1	5.2	28.7	1.7	10.6	8.7	100.0	576
Entertainment	29.1	4.5	34.4	18.8	5.0	8.3	100.0	581
Business/Jobs	77.4	1.7	4.4	0.2	3.3	13.1	100.0	543

[3]Refers to relatives, neighbors, friends, colleagues, etc.

of the respondents consider newspapers as the most useful source (Table 28); the figures for television, radio, personal sources, movies and magazines are 17.4 percent, 8.0 percent, 5.2 percent, 0.2 percent, and 1.4 percent respectively. For information on business and jobs, the most useful medium is newspapers (77.4%), followed by personal sources (13.1%), television (4.4%), magazines (3.3%), and radio (1.7%).

Newspapers are considered by 48.8 percent of the respondents to be the most reliable source among the mass media, followed by television (25.7%), personal sources (8.9%), magazines (8.2%), radio (5.9%), and movies (2.5%).

As shown in Table 29, newspapers are considered the most reliable source for all types of information, but not for entertainment. For both entertainment and sports, television is a very reliable source of information. Magazines are a reliable source for information on health and nutrition, and education. Personal sources are thought to be reliable for information on health and nutrition, and business and jobs. Movies are reliable only for entertainment.

For information on government policies and public affairs, 61.1 percent of the respondents indicated that newspapers are the most reliable source, followed by television (23.4%), radio (9.9%), personal sources (4.4%), and magazines (1.2%). More Malays consider television to be the most reliable source for information on government policies and public affairs than the Chinese and the Indians. More Indians consider radio the most reliable source than other ethnic groups. Regarding information on business and economic affairs, 76.9 percent of the respondents indicated that newspapers are the most reliable source of information, 13.3 percent indicated personal sources, 4.4 percent indicated television, 4.1 percent indicated movies and magazines.

Table 29

Respondents Who Believe the Various Media to Be the Most Reliable Source, by Type of Information (percent)

Types of Information	News-paper	Radio	TV	Movie	Magazine	Personal Source	Total %	Total N
Govt. Policies/ Public Affairs	61.1	9.9	23.4	0.0	1.2	4.4	100.0	589
International/ Current Events	59.2	7.1	24.5	0.0	6.6	2.6	100.0	579
Health/Nutrition	27.1	8.5	17.7	0.2	24.2	22.3	100.0	575
Sports	44.1	4.8	42.7	0.4	4.4	3.6	100.0	522
Education	44.8	4.9	29.8	0.7	11.3	6.5	100.0	574
Entertainment	27.7	5.5	37.7	15.9	5.5	7.7	100.0	578
Business/Jobs	76.9	0.9	4.4	0.4	4.1	13.3	100.0	541

5

Communication Policies and Laws

The relevance of communication policies to the actual operation and functioning of the communication system in a society is best summarized by Sommerlad:

> The ways in which communication is used, the networks through which it flows, the structures of the media system, the regulatory framework for the system, and the decisions of people who operate it, are all the outcome of communication policies. Policies are the principles, rules and guidelines on which the system is built and may be specifically formulated or remain largely implicit. (Sommerlad 1975, p. 7)

In our discussion of the guiding communication policies in Singapore, we will adopt the definition by Unesco which sees communication policies as sets of social norms "established to guide the behavior of communication systems" (quoted in Rahim 1977, p. 13). We will focus especially on the normative guidelines, formulated by the political leaders, that are actually being implemented through legal and institutional constraints to "guide the behavior of communication systems" (Rahim 1977, p. 13). According to J. Lee (1976, p. 33), "National policy involves decisions on the institutionalization of communication media and functions. It also entails control to an extent which ensures that these institutions' operations are directed towards the public good."

Communication Policies

Generally, the People's Action Party leaders in Singapore perceive mass media as powerful instruments that can guide the masses. The audience, on the other hand, is persuasible and can hardly resist the influence of the mass media. Based on these assumptions, two propositions are deduced: First, mass media, if in the "wrong" hands, may be abused to disrupt the social harmony and political stability of the society. And second, mass media, with proper guidance, can perform a constructive role in nation-building, especially in developing countries. Mass media communication is therefore a "double-edged weapon," as Mr. Jek Yeun Thong, then Minister for Culture, put it in 1971 (*The Mirror,* September 20, 1971). Logically, the above propositions lead to the conclusion that the operation of the mass media must be properly controlled and supervised.

A review of parliamentary records and speeches made by government leaders since Singapore achieved self-government in 1959 reveals that the political leaders have been consistent in their views about the freedom of the press and role of the mass media, although some slight twist in emphasis is observable over the years.

The Constitution of Singapore, like most constitutions in countries throughout the world, guarantees that every citizen has the right to freedom of speech and expression. Such freedom, in Singapore as in any other country, is never absolute. In a speech to the University of Singapore Law Society in January 1962, Prime Minister Lee Kuan Yew made this point clear: "The rule of law talks of *habeas corpus,* freedom, the right of association and expression, of assembly, of peaceful demonstration . . . . But nowhere in the world today are these rights allowed to practise without limitations, for blindly applied, these ideals can work towards the undoing of organised society" (Singapore Government Press Statement, January 19, 1963).

During the early years after self-government, when the PAP government was still confronted by opposition MPs in the parliament, the leaders were compelled to define explicitly the limitations of such freedom. Mr. Rajaratnam, then Minister for Culture and an ex-journalist, was among the first tc do that. In a parliamentary session, he pointed out that:

> If a newspaper indulges in tactics which might incite communal hatred or race riots, we will intervene. In fact, during the last one year, we have had occasion to ring up the Press and ask for their cooperation to keep certain unpleasant stories out of the Press . . . when we think that the interest of the country as a whole is involved, then, to that extent, we are quite prepared to modify the absolute freedom, which nobody accepts, not even in Britain. To that extent, . . . we concede that we do interfere with the Press. (*Singapore Legislative Assembly Debates,* Vol. 14, 1960-1961, Col. 547–548)

Issues and problems relating to ethnic relations and communal conflicts are therefore considered as sensitive areas to be treated with great care. Another taboo topic involves pro-Communist opinions and activities. As Mr. Ong Pang Boon, then Minister for Home Affairs, once put it: "Our policy in this respect is generally like this. All publications in praise of the Communist way of life and advocating unconstitutional means to overthrow the government and publications of a purely propaganda nature must, of course, be banned and will continue to be banned." (*Singapore Legislative Assembly Debates,* Vol. 15, 1961, Col. 2040)

After Singapore's independence in 1965, and as the PAP control became more stabilized, government leaders began to put more emphasis on the positive role of mass media in national development. This was stated as a guiding policy of the Ministry of Culture. According to Jek Yeun Thong, then Minister for Culture:

> In the mass media aspect of our activity, it is our policy (i.e., the Ministry of Culture) to induce the change of attitudes in our people. Many a developing country has rightly endeavoured to modernise itself on the basis of economic and social transformation but has inadvertently omitted a vital area—the minds of men. Our modernisation process should never neglect attitudinal change in our people and this is where the mass media come in to play an essential role. (*Singapore Parliamentary Debates,* Vol. 27, 1968, Col. 190–191)

Prime Minister Mr. Lee Kuan Yew once pointed out that the mass media can take initiative and positively support government programs and policies:

> The mass media can help to present Singapore's problems simply and clearly and then explain how if they support certain programmes and policies these problems can be solved. More important, we want the mass media to reinforce, not to undermine, the cultural values and social attitudes being inculcated in our schools and universities. (*The Mirror,* June 14, 1971)

Several incidents involving the press happened in 1971 in Singapore. The *Eastern Sun* and the *Singapore Herald* were closed for alleged foreign funding and control. Earlier in the same year, four top executives of *Nanyang Siang Pau* were detained on charges of "glamourizing the communist way of life" and trying "to stir Chinese racial emotion." These incidents naturally caused concern and criticism both locally and internationally. To defend his policy, Mr. Lee Kuan Yew made a revealing speech to the general assembly of the International Press Institute at Helsinki in June 1971:

> The Singapore Government has the responsibility to neutralise the attempts of foreign agencies and communists to make political gains by shaping opinions and attitudes of Singaporeans . . . . In such a situation, . . . freedom of the press, freedom of news media, must

> be subordinated to the overriding needs of the integrity of Singapore, and to the primacy of purpose of an elected government. (*The Mirror,* June 14, 1971)

The fear of foreign control of local mass media has since become a common theme and has been presented as a legitimate reason for imposing political control and stringent legal constraints on communication systems in Singapore. The same concern was readily echoed by other government leaders in the early 1970s. Here is an example of such statements:

> There are insidious external forces which seek to manipulate public opinion so as to weaken our national will and make our Government more pliable to their wishes. The mass media are particularly susceptible to such manipulation. We should not confuse actions taken by Government to preserve the autonomy of Singapore with the denial of freedom of the press. (Dr. Augustine Tan, MP, University economist and then Political Secretary to PM, *Singapore Parliamentary Debates*, Vol. 31, 1971-1972, Col. 82)

Foreign influences need not take the form of direct control of ownership of local mass media. Such external influences may be unintentional but nevertheless effective as a form of cultural imperialism. Ironically, Singapore is especially susceptible to such cultural invasion because of its relatively well-developed communication system and frequent contact with the outside world. As Mr. Lee Kuan Yew puts it, "We are an international junction for ships, aircraft and telecommunications by cable and satellite. People from the richer countries of the West, their magazines, newspapers, television, and cinema films, all come in. We are very exposed. It is impossible to insulate Singaporeans from the outside world." This situation justifies the need for censorship. But "censorship can only partially cut off these influences. It is more crucial that local production of films and publication of newspapers should not be surreptitiously captured by their proxies." (*The Mirror,* June 14, 1971)

The same concern was reiterated by Mr. Jek Yeun Thong, then Minister for Culture, in his speech to the Commonwealth Broadcasting Association meeting in 1976. He indicated that concern about the influences of broadcast satellites and communications technology centered on two issues: "The first is the imbalance in the flow of TV films from the technologically advanced countries which control the production and distribution of these films. The second concerns the influence which this one-way flow of TV films can exert on the receiving countries . . ." He suggests two ways to solve these problems: one is to "ensure cultural pluralism in TV programmes with less air time and a judicious selection of programmes . . ." and the other is "to be culturally self-reliant where each country produces most of its television programmes" (*The Mirror,* October 11, 1976). Obviously, in Singapore the first alternative has been adopted as part of the broadcasting policy with regard to the imbalance of the flow of programs.

One of the consistent themes regarding communication policies in Singapore is the government's and leaders' views on the "relativeness" of freedom of the press. The unique socio-cultural and political situation of the society thus justifies the special form and boundaries of freedom of the press applied to it. According to Jek Yeun Thong,

> Singapore has never had freedom of the press as it is understood in the Western world .... It is ... futile to try to draw a comparison between the case of *The New York Times* and the case of the newspapers in Singapore .... In the first place, we do not have such traditions (of freedom of the press). In the second place, in the United States riots can happen every day and everywhere, and yet the country remains stable and prosperous. But in Singapore, one bloody riot will wreck the whole country. (*Singapore Parliamentary Debates,* Vol. 31, 1971-1972, Col. 216-217)

More recently, the view that freedom of the press in a society is relative rather than absolute was reiterated by the Prime Minister when he commented on the human rights issue championed by President Carter of the United States: "We have got to hope that [President Carter's] measures are sufficiently practical to be able to take into account the different historic, cultural and value systems of different parts of the world in different stages of development" (*Straits Times,* May 26, 1977). In another interview with a foreign correspondent, Lee asked, "Can we and must we all accept the same moral standards, or human rights? Or like varying dress styles have they really evolved over different historic, cultural, climatic and technological circumstances" (*Straits Times,* May 17, 1977).

While freedom is relative, a line somehow should still be drawn between an open society and a closed society. It is thus significant that Lee expressed his vision of an open society in the same interview. In his view, "as long as there is freedom of access to information about what is going on in the world and you can read more than what the Government puts out, that is an essential part of the ingredient to the open society" (*Straits Times,* May 17, 1977). This statement may be seen to represent the lower limit to freedom of the press that the Singapore government will maintain in its policies regarding communication activities.

Communication Laws

Based on the assumption that media communication is powerful as educational and persuasive instruments, two guiding principles deduced regarding media communication activities are: First, in the passive sense, media communication should be properly controlled or supervised so that it will not be abused against the national interest. Second, in the active sense, media communication should be properly used to assist in nation-building and social development. These guiding policy principles have been translated into acts, statutes, and regulations in Singapore. Some of these laws are specifically designed to regulate the operation of certain types of media, while others are more pervasive, affecting communication and information activities in general.

According to legal acts, several communication media are put directly under the government control as part of government operation within the bureaucratic structure. Thus, the Post Office Act (1947) puts the operation of postal services under the jurisdiction of the Postal Services Department, within the Ministry of Communication, in the same way as the Telecommunication Authority of Singapore (Telecom) was created to have total control of telephone, telex, telegraph, and satellite communications (see chapter 3).

Likewise, by means of the licensing and other requirements described in chapter 3, radio and television broadcasting are under the direct control of the government to interpret and promote government policies for nation-building objectives.

Legal constraints on the operation of newspapers are less direct. The new Newspaper and Printing Act of 1974, stirred up some heated discussion and criticism because it gives the government the right to grant and withdraw licenses for the operation of printing presses in Singapore. (This is a constraint on all publications, rather than just newspapers.) According to the Act, all newspapers in Singapore have to be published by newspaper companies in which:

1. A permit is granted, and must be reviewed annually;
2. All the directors are Singapore citizens;
3. There are two types of shares: ordinary and management shares; and
4. No management shares may be issued or transferred except to Singapore citizens and corporations which have been granted specific approval by the government. Every management share carries two hundred votes in any resolution relating to the appointment or dismissal of any director or member of the staff of the newspaper company.

Reflecting concern about the possibility of foreign control, the law also stipulates that a newspaper or a journalist is prohibited from receiving foreign funds without the approval of the government. According to Jek Yeun Thong,

> Management will be free to operate the newspapers as commercial enterprises, provided they ensure that there is no manipulation by foreign elements and that no attempt is made by them, or through their proxies,

> to glorify undesirable viewpoints and philosophies. (*Singapore Parliamentary Debates*, Vol. 33, 1974, Col. 914)

In 1977, a new constraint was imposed on the ownership of newspaper shares with the passing of the Newspaper and Printing Presses (Amendment) Bill. The bill prohibits any person from holding either directly or indirectly, through a nominee or a holding company, more than three percent of the ordinary shares issued by the newspaper company. According to Jek Yeun Thong,

> It is undesirable to allow any person or family to have monopolistic control of any major newspaper. In view of the great influence the news media has on public opinion and the possibilities of it being used to manipulate weaker elements in an open society like Singapore, it is essential to spread the ownership of newspapers as widely as possible. (*Singapore Parliamentary Debates,* Vol. 37, 1977–1978, Col. 67)

Film censorship, according to the Cinematographic Films Act (1954), is the responsibility of the Board of Film Censors, which is under the jurisdiction of the Ministry of Culture. There is no system of film classification in existence in Singapore, although the issue has recently been brought up for discussion. The Board of Film Censors is responsible for the censorship of films of all lengths and types and film accessories which includes: posters, handbills, pressbooks, newspapers, film advertisements, catch-lines, color transparencies, still photographs, videotapes and cassette films. Films may be approved in total or with alterations or excisions. According to the Ministry of Culture, films may be banned for various reasons, such as "the glorification of gangsterism, violence, crime, hippism, free love, promiscuity, homosexuality, lesbianism, incest, permissiveness, religious prejudice and racism." Films are also banned for "political reasons" (*Singapore Parliamentary Debates,* Vol. 32, 1973, Col. 1089). The Board banned a total of 73 films in 1976. Out of these, 55 percent were banned for glorifying crime, violence, gangsterism or drug addiction; 32 percent involved sex exploitation or were morally objectionable; 12 percent were banned for political reasons and the rest on religious grounds (*Straits Times,* March 21, 1977). In 1977, a total of 84 films were banned; about 45 percent because of crime and violence, 35 percent because of sexual exploitation, and the rest were for political and religious reasons (*Sin Chew Jit Poh,* February 5, 1978).

Several legal acts are applied to communication activities in general and are therefore more profound in their constraining power. These include the Undesirable Publications Act (1967), which prohibits the importation, sale, or circulation of publications published or printed outside or within Singapore that are considered "contrary to the public interest." The Ministry of Culture is authorized to administer the Act. Other than the vague definition of undesirable publications being those judged "contrary to the public interest," there has been no public revelation of the criteria applied by the Ministry in the implementation of the Act. Four broad categories have, however, been identified: politically offensive, morally offensive, religiously offensive, and ethnically offensive (Bryd 1970, p. 67).

The Sedition Act (1964) prohibits behavior including speeches, publications, and distribution or circulation of publications with "seditious tendency." In this case, "a seditious tendency" is legally defined as a tendency:

(a) to bring into hatred or contempt or to excite disaffection against the government;
(b) to excite the citizens of Singapore or the residents in Singapore to attempt to procure in Singapore, the alteration, otherwise than by lawful means, of any matter as by law established;
(c) to bring into hatred or contempt or to excite disaffection against the administration of justice in Singapore;
(d) to raise discontent or disaffection amongst the citizens of Singapore or the residents in Singapore; and
(e) to promote feelings of ill-will and hostility between different races or classes of the population of Singapore. (*Singapore Statutes,* Revised Edition 1970, Chapter 106)

Another basic—and probably the most controversial—legislative act which affects the mass media in Singapore is the Internal Security Act (1963) which confers wide-ranging powers on the executive to fight subversion and to repel security threats. The Minister for Home Affairs is authorized to prohibit the printing, publication, sale, issue, circulation, or possession of a document or publication deemed prejudicial to the national interest, public order, or society of Singapore.

The Public Entertainments Act (l959) requires that public entertainment can be provided only in an approved place, and in accordance with a license issued by the Licensing Officer. In this Act, public entertainment is defined to include, among others, performing arts, exhibitions, sporting contests and trade fairs.

The Emergency (Essential Powers) Act (1964) prohibits all members of the Singapore armed forces from communicating with newspapers. Any matter which discredits the Singapore military, or constitutes a grievance against a member's position is also prohibited from being discussed. The law specifies that if a member of the Singapore armed forces does communicate with any editor, proprietor, manager, printer, or employee of a newspaper and that newspaper publishes the content of the complaint, the newspaper management is required to divulge the identity of the complaining member of the armed forces if the Ministry of National Defense so requests.

Under the Prohibition on Advertisements Relating to Smoking Act (1970), no advertising relating to the use of cigarettes, cigars, or tobacco is permitted. Another legal regulation on advertising activites is the

Medicines (Medical Advertisements) Regulations (1977) which requires that a permit from the Ministry of Health must be obtained to advertise medicinal products, apparatus, or any device.

Freedom and Responsibility

The existence of the above-mentioned laws and their efficient enforcement means that the government of Singapore can effectively, directly or indirectly, control and utilize the mass communication system to pursue its defined objectives of nation-building. This makes it possible for the Prime Minister to become a "tutor-politician," using "the mass media...to take the whole nation into a collective tutorial on the problems of politics" (Thomson 1974, p. 25). An American political scientist has observed that:

> The PAP inaugurated a policy of information saturation to educate, convert, give shape to, and guide public opinion. The emphasis on political communication, which has accelerated over the years, evinces an abiding belief in the efficacy of information, argumentation, and reason to establish and confirm popular support for the government. This policy also manifests a PAP conviction that the common man possesses a substantial rational streak which will generally lead him to support a policy which can be presented and defended as factually and logically correct. This conviction is integral to PAP thinking. (Bellows 1970, pp. 46-47)

As a result, the communication pattern in Singapore is characterized by a largely one-way flow from the leadership to the masses with government and media people at various levels serving as gatekeepers. The contents of media are often persuasive and educational, as well as being informational and entertaining, reflecting the paternalistic political structure in Singapore.

Under the circumstances, the mass media system often fails to become an effective channel for political articulation and participation by the general public. As Thomson puts it, "Our mass media have not generally been prime political initiating agents in themselves, as were newspapers in other countries" (1974, p. 25). The feedback information in the national communication system relies basically on the government's own established institutional channels such as the citizens' consultative committees and the management committees of the community centers (Chan 1975, p. 55). To a limited extent, the letters-to-the-editor sections of the newspapers also serve as a forum for public opinion articulation. As Chan puts it, "this kind of political action is permissible for not having organization and action behind it; it is not viewed as disruptive." But articulation through those columns can only be on limited issues concerning "the demand for a better and more efficient administration rather than an argument on values and goals" (Chan 1975, p. 56; see also Neo 1978).

This appears to be a concern shared not only among academics, but also among some media practitioners and government leaders. Goh Kian Chee, a *Straits Times* journalist, pointed out in late 1977 that there is a problem of getting a rational and open debate on important public issues. He indicated that the mass media could play a crucial role in encouraging a freer atmosphere for debate. Newspapers could provide more relevant news, better local and international coverage and go into areas imagined by cautious editors to be out of bounds.

> The danger is that if these improvements are not made soon, the alternative is the creation of a semi-mindless, undiscerning Singaporean readership or viewership which can be easily misled in a political contest into emotional and hysterical responses. (*Straits Times,* December 29, l977)

Under the watchful eye of the government, careful self-censorship by cautious editors is known to be a common practice. While the incidence and extent of self-censorship by local media cannot be documented, several incidents involving foreign news magazines have been reported and are revealing.

In March 1977, an issue of the *Far Eastern Economic Review* was withheld from circulation by its distributor. The distributor took the cautious step despite an assurance by the Ministry of Culture that it had no objection to the circulation of that issue. The cause of concern in that issue was that some replies by the *Review's* editor to certain charges by the Singapore government might constitute libel (*Straits Times,* March 22, 1977).

Another reported case of self-censorship involved an issue of *Time* magazine in August 1977. The issue included a two-column article entitled "Singapore—Tight Little Island" about alleged governmental "muzzling" of the press. The issue was circulated in Singapore with one sentence (26 words) heavily daubed with black ink. A spokesman for the distributor of *Time* magazine in Singapore told the reporter that "We censored the article ourselves on the advice of our lawyers" (*Straits Times,* August 8, 1977). The regional manager of *Time* also commented: "*Time* is quite often censored either in part or in total. There is nothing unusual about this incident" (*Straits Times,* August 8, 1977).

In Singapore, the mass media people perform their roles as depicted by the government and by their own professional codes. Constrained by various proscriptions and prescriptions, their job is important and challenging, but never easy. As Chan puts it:

> The extent to which the newspapers can become a major channel of the articulation of public problems

depends to a large extent on the newspapers themselves, for ultimately it is the editors who determine the limits of debate and they, of course, in turn are affected by the knowledge that pursuing an issue too determinedly can be construed as anti-national as the editors of *Nanyang Siang Pau* and the *Singapore Herald* discovered. (Chan 1975, p. 56)

6

Social Policy Planning in Singapore

Planning, according to Waterston (1965, p. 26), is in essence "an organized, conscious and continual attempt to select the best available alternatives to achieve specific goals." When applied to society, "planning is the rationalization of political decisions; it is the use of knowledge to maximize existing means toward the achievement of given goals" (Benveniste 1968, p. 29). Social planning therefore involves a strategy or strategies expressed and implemented as social policies to change the society or the existing social system either in part or in totality into a more desired state (cf. L. Chong 1974, p. 6). In this sense, social planning includes planning for both economic and noneconomic development of a society, although in many developing countries including Singapore most planning efforts have been dedicated to the economic aspect of social development. As a result, more information is available on activities relating to economic planning.

In this chapter, we will discuss aspects of social policy planning in Singapore, to identify the major planning units and the characteristics of social planning. There are three types of social planning: general development planning, urban development planning, and communication planning.

Strategy of Social Policy Planning

Singapore, unlike many developing countries, has not had a formal overall development plan since 1960–1964, when its First Five-Year Plan was adopted and published spelling out social and economic priorities and programs. Ironically, "this period, as many sceptics of formal planning are fond of pointing out, had the lowest growth rates ever experienced by Singapore in the last fifteen years" (Pang, forthcoming).

The first development plan was formulated soon after the People's Action Party was elected in 1959 and was prepared within the Ministry of Finance, based on proposals submitted by various government departments and ministries (S. Lee 1973, p. 32). The plan came at a time when the problem of unemployment was paramount in Singapore's economy, as a result of the rapid population increase after World War II. The government's most urgent task was to draw up plans to expand industrialization and promote export-oriented industries to provide jobs for the backlog of unemployed persons as well as for the young school leavers. The Plan addressed itself to the various problems then facing Singapore:

1. The creation of employment opportunities for the children, born in the post-World War II years, who would be seeking employment in the 1960s;
2. The provision of adequate housing and secondary education, which were also consequences of the baby boom; and
3. The raising of revenue and loans to fund capital expenditure over a medium-term period (S. Lee 1973, p. 7).

A second development plan was prepared for the period 1966–1970, but because of events during the late 1960s it had to be revised and was subsequently abandoned. That plan was never officially published. According to Singapore's Economic Planning Unit (Second Development Plan 1966–1970, quoted in L. Chong 1974, p. 187),

> The objectives of the Second Plan have been formulated in the contexts of the long term aims of economic and social development which were clearly enunciated in the formulation of the First Plan. These aims can be briefly stated as follows: (1) to transform the economic structure of the Republic by promoting the growth of the industrial sector to complement the traditional entrepôt trading sector; (2) to generate sufficient new employment opportunities for the new entrants to the labour force; and (3) to provide a satisfactory level of social services particularly in education, health and housing.

One major event that led to the scrapping of the Second Plan was the shock announcement in late 1966 that the British would withdraw their forces from Singapore completely by the end of 1971. "This gave the Singapore government barely five years to build up a local defense capability or partake in a regional defense arrangement" (S. Lee 1973, p. 21). According to the finance minister, Mr. Hon Sui Sen,

> The Second Development Plan 1966–1970, prepared after separation from Malaysia, had hardly been set for printing when the shock announcement of the British military rundown changed the premises upon which the Plan was based. The uncertainties engendered by these adverse factors had their major effects upon our promotion plans for attracting manufacturing industry, which we had intensified as a key development sector

required to solve the problems of increasing unemployment. (Hon 1973, p. 20)

As things turned out, industrial growth was not much of a problem in the late 1960s because of the capital inflow from Hong Kong following the Chinese Cultural Revolution in 1966. The problem was rather, as pointed out by S. Lee (1973, p. 21), the shortage of technically-trained labor. The Second Plan had to be revised to put greater emphasis on technical education.

Another event was the monetary split which occurred between Malaysia and Singapore in 1967 over how the assets of the Currency Board were to be legally held and reflected a lack of mutual confidence and trust following political separation in 1965. Singapore was more dependent on overseas capital for the smooth functioning of its trading economy and had to build up external confidence in her currency (S. Lee 1973, p. 21).

By the time all the adjustments and modifications were made in the Second Plan, the government had decided to abandon formal planning totally and rely on ad hoc or year-to-year rolling plans. Such plans were announced yearly in the finance minister's annual budget statements, with each year's plans formulated to complement and supplement those of the previous year (Seah 1976, p. 22). Thus, since the mid-sixties Singapore's economic development has been characterized by a lack of formal economic planning. There is neither a central planning agency nor a long-term plan for economic development. The rolling plans are considered by Seah (and others) to be more suitable in the Singapore context:

> A rolling plan is more flexible, and could provide for the continuous revision of the planning framework as and when new information and events come by. Such ad hoc plans suited the Singapore economic structure as well as the government's philosophy of pragmatic socialism. The PAP government has always advocated pragmatism and flexibility in its policies, and is quick to respond to opportunities and events. (Seah 1976, p. 22)

According to Pang, the hallmark of the Singapore planning style is flexibility both in initiating required changes and in responding to new problems. "The political leadership develops the social and economic strategies . . . paying appropriate attention to their political costs. Policy implementation is normally left to executive government agencies. But it is not unusual for the Cabinet itself to be involved in settling coordination problems which arise when a policy has to be implemented jointly by several public agencies" (Pang, forthcoming).

Economically, and to a lesser extent, politically and socially, Singapore is highly vulnerable and susceptible to changes in external conditions. This makes long-term planning meaningless. "In other words, since outside events and changes greatly affect domestic conditions, forecasting and adherence to fixed targets in formal planning become futile as well as disastrous" (Seah 1976, p. 22).

Several reasons have been given to explain the success in social and economic development in Singapore without long-term formal planning. One is the continuity of the PAP government in Singapore since 1959.

> The Singapore government system combines centralization at the top level of decision-making with a fair degree of de-centralization at the next lower operating level. The result is that key cabinet members are in constant personal touch with each other, exchanging information, debating and arbitrating points of issues, co-ordinating programmes and issuing directives to the next level of authority. In other words, the leadership has taken over a variety of functions which are usually left to the central planning agency (Seah, 1976, p. 22).

Or, as Fawcett and Chen (forthcoming) put it, in Singapore "intragovernment coordination is fairly strong, largely because of the relatively small number of people in policymaking positions and their frequent interactions, and the planning mechanism is flexible enough to respond to changing conditions."

The small size of the country, and the economy, permits easier coordination and implementation of development projects without long-term formal planning. The compactness of Singapore also means that there is no need for regional planning, nor are there agricultural and industrial sectors to be coordinated or balanced.

Development Planning and Policymaking

Administratively, the cabinet is the highest agency with power to make national development policies. It is responsible for overall administration and for providing parliament with policy on which to base decisions. In secret cabinet meetings all important points of ministerial and departmental policies are discussed and courses of action decided. Responsibility for the implementation of policies is delegated to the appropriate ministries, departments, and statutory boards.

Since the details of cabinet meetings are not revealed, very little information is publicly known and documented about the processes by which decisions are made on national development policies and programs. Cabinet deliberations are not reported in the press, and meetings of government advisory committees are in most cases conducted in private. Nor are special interest groups normally invited by the government to present their views on impending policies. According to Fawcett and Chen (forthcoming),

> The style of the government is to treat consideration of policy alternatives as an "in-house" matter, rather than as a matter for public discussion. Typically, then, information about policy formulation is available only after the fact, at which point the information to be disclosed is a matter of government choice.

It is thus apparent that the study of public policy planning in Singapore is subject to significant constraints as the information available is fragmentary and limited in scope.

Because there is no formal centralized planning body in Singapore, planning and implementation are carried out by the various ministries or their departments, boards, or other affiliated bodies, all of them having access to the cabinet through the ministers who are also cabinet members.

Ministerial committees are formed to be responsible for planning and coordination on specific problems. Several such committees are known to exist. In 1965, a ministerial committee was established to secure more effective and better-coordinated physical planning and development control in the state. The committee was chaired by the prime minister and the ministers for Finance, Law, and National Development were members (*Singapore Parliamentary Debates,* 1965, Vol. 24, Col. 29–30). In 1968, it was also announced that the government had set up a cabinet committee comprising the ministers for Education, Labour, and Finance "to look into the problem and to supervise the planning and implementation of technical education and vocational training. This is to avoid any possible duplication in planning and implementation of technical education and vocational training, and to ensure that they correspond with our manpower needs and employment opportunities" (*Singapore Parliamentary Debates,* 1968, Vol. 27, Col. 181). It is understood that other ministerial committees are also formed to deal with specific subjects for more effective inter-ministerial planning and coordination.

Before 1969, an overall development-related project was the Economic Planning Unit (EPU) established in 1963 to serve as a central planning agency. It was initially organized within the prime minister's office and was transferred to the Ministry of Finance in 1966. Among the first tasks of the EPU were a review of the implementation of the First Five-Year Plan and preparation for the second development plan (S. Lee 1973, p. 32).

According to S. Lee (1973), the EPU was basically concerned with processing department proposals or ideas from statutory boards for public development expenditures. The EPU, after processing a project proposal and then only after it was satisfied with the case, would send up the entire proposal to the three members of the cabinet who constituted the Development Planning Committee—the ministers for Finance, Law, and National Development, and the department which originated the proposal. The committee did not meet formally to deliberate on each project, but the documents relating to the project were simply considered by each member in turn. Only when there was unanimous approval from all three members would the project be included in the development budget (S. Lee 1973, pp. 33–34).

In 1969, the EPU was dissolved and its staff absorbed by other departments, mainly the Project Division of the Economic Development Board and the Development Division of the Ministry of Finance.

Today, the Development Division of the Ministry of Finance is the key government department which monitors all aspects of development policy planning. The division prepares quarterly and annual economic reports and scrutinizes project proposals to see if they conform with development priorities and with the rolling five-year public sector development plan. Such proposals are then submitted to the Development Planning Committee which approves development projects in the public sector. The Development Planning Committee thus functions as the policymaking unit of the government, with the Development Division of the Ministry of Finance acting as its secretariat; the Budget Division of the Ministry of Finance also examines proposals for budgetary soundness (Pang, forthcoming).

Generally, planning for social and economic development in Singapore is done on a short-term basis in accordance with development priorities set by the government. The planning rationale is basically project-oriented. A project is initiated to deal with some well-defined objectives, and such projects can be initiated by a ministry, a department, or a statutory board, or may be a response to a directive from the Cabinet.

As planning in Singapore is pragmatic and project-oriented, statutory boards play a very crucial role. A statutory board is established with specific functions—to tackle defined problems and to achieve required targets. For example, when the Singapore government chose industrialization as a top development priority in the early 1960s, the Economic Development Board (EDB) was established in 1961 to promote industrialization and economic development. Similarly, the Housing and Development Board (HDB) was established in 1960 to undertake large-scale public housing programs to solve the acute housing problems in Singapore. The Singapore Family Planning and Population Board (SFPPB) was established in 1966 to launch comprehensive family planning programs. Another example is the setting up of the National Wages Council (NWC) in 1973, to regulate wage increases in both the public and private sectors in order that wage increases might be matched by an increase in labor productivity.

At present, there are nearly ninety statutory bodies. About one third of these are public services boards, and the other two thirds are advisory and regulatory boards.

Although each statutory body is responsible for solving a defined set of problems and achieving certain goals, programs to achieve those goals are not simply formulated and implemented by the statutory board concerned. Once the policy is accepted as national policy, cooperation from all related government bodies to ensure the success of the program is expected. For instance, the bilingual education policy is a national policy. Achievement of this goal is not merely the responsibility of the Ministry of Education but is also the task of Radio Television Singapore (RTS), the Ministry of Culture, the Ministry of Defense, the Ministry of Labour and other related ministries. Cooperation from all related government bodies is assured.

Another example is family planning and population control. Although the Singapore Family Planning and Population Board (SFPPB) was established with the specific task of ensuring the success of the national family planning programs, many population policies and social measures regulating family size are introduced and implemented by various government bodies over which the board has no control.

A good example of public-policy planning in Singapore is the formulation of future population policies. In April 1976 to formulate policies for the next ten years, the Ministry of Health and the SFPPB convened a two-day closed-door colloquium to discuss the problems and the tasks to be achieved. The colloquium was attended by the minister for Health, the chairman of the SFPPB, the permanent secretaries or deputy secretaries of most ministries, and the chairmen of some statutory boards, who together worked out and endorsed the basic guidelines for future family planning programs and population policies.

The success of this type of planning depends mainly on the cooperation and coordination of the various government bodies at the implementation stage. Again, the compactness of the society and the strong and stable leadership facilitate smooth coordination in implementing national policies in Singapore.

Urban Development Planning[4]

Because Singapore is a small, densely populated city-state urban planning is a very important part of social planning there. The responsibility for urban development and urban planning belongs to the Ministry of National Development, which handles public and middle-income housing, urban renewal, public works, primary production, and parks and recreation. It regulates or controls state and city planning, development and building, land use, car parks, and import/export of agricultural and animal produce. Project proposals are prepared by the ministry and submitted to the Cabinet for evaluation and final approval through the procedures described above. The approved policies and projects are carried out by the Housing and Development Board, the Urban Redevelopment Authority, and three departments, namely, Public Works, Primary Production, and Planning (Ministry of Culture 1976, p. 75).

Two long-term comprehensive urban development plans, the Master Plan and the Concept Plan, have been formulated as guidelines for drafting specific project plans.

As early as 1918, a commission was set up by the British colonial

[4]A part of this section is discussed in P. Chen (1976-77).

government to study the problems of overcrowding and inadequate housing in Singapore. However, Singapore did not have overall physical planning for urban development until 1958, when a Master Plan was approved by the colonial government. It was replaced by the Concept Plan in the early 1970s.

During the colonial period, urban planning in Singapore was limited to what could be achieved through control of private development by regulations governing building and land subdivision, and through the Singapore Improvement Trust, which was established in 1927. Squatter settlements and shacks were built during the period of Japanese occupation. The situation deteriorated when previous town dwellers rushed back from their hiding in the countryside in Singapore and Malaya at the end of World War II. At the same time, there was a big inflow of migrants from China and India. The population problem became more serious under the pressure of a high birth rate and rural-urban migration, accelerated by the emergency in Malaya in the 1950s. Overcrowding and the housing shortage became increasingly acute.

The preparation of the Master Plan commenced in 1951 and it was approved by the colonial government in 1958; it was the first comprehensive physical development plan for the whole island of Singapore. The plan covered the 20-year period from 1953 to 1972. The machinery for implementation of the Master Plan was spelled out in the Planning Ordinance of 1959, which went into operation in 1960 and was administered by the Planning Department in the Ministry of Law and National Development—later the Ministry of National Development when the former ministry was split into two.

Generally, the core policy for urban development as reflected in the Master Plan was one of decentralization. The growth of the existing city was to be limited by a green belt; the population living in the central city was to be reduced by one-sixth to alleviate problems of overcrowding and traffic congestion; and further urban growth was to be accommodated in three new towns some distance from the central city.

The Master Plan reflects, however, the rather conservative thinking and limited aspirations of the colonial government, which at that time could not foresee the rapid political and economic changes that followed self-government in 1959. It soon became clear that a new comprehensive plan was needed to provide guidelines for physical planning under the new social and demographic conditions. In 1967, the Singapore government undertook a major planning project to prepare another long-range comprehensive urban development plan with the assistance of the United Nations Development Program (UNDP).

The government set up an ad hoc organization known as the State and City Planning Office within the Ministry of Law and National Development. The office was staffed by officers seconded from the Planning Department, the Traffic Unit of the Public Works Department, the Housing and Development Board, and by others specially recruited for the project.

The terms of reference for the project, among others, were:

1. The collection of the data required to support both comprehensive and project planning;
2. The preparation of a long-range, comprehensive physical development plan for Singapore;
3. The preparation of a policy sketch plan for urban renewal of the Central Area; and
4. Assistance in developing the resources of the Planning Department to enable it to undertake the comprehensive planning of a large and complex city on a continuing basis.

The project was completed in October 1971, with the production of the Concept Plan, which was projected to 1992, a period of 20 years. The design was for Singapore to accommodate a population of 3.4 to 4 million—more than the projected population of 2.7 to 2.9 million for 1995, based on present demographic statistics.

The Concept Plan deals mainly with the distribution of major activities, expressed as predominant land uses, and organized in terms of transportation links between structural units within a system. There is a proposed system of expressways, major arterial roads, airports, major new service centers, a mass transit system, large land-consuming industries, overall settlement patterns for housing of high and low densities, and an open space system.

The Concept Plan provides guidelines for overall planning and policy for urban and environmental development in Singapore. The plan will explicitly and implicitly affect, if not forcefully determine, patterns of ecological distribution of the population, public and private housing estates, and industrial estates anywhere on the island.

The existence of the overall comprehensive plans makes the planning of specific urban development projects relatively easy. (It should be noted however that the latter also go through the same processes of cabinet evaluation and approval as other development projects.) The role of the Ministry of National Development as the central organization for urban planning permits better coordination and more effective implementation. This is a contrast to the fragmentary state of communication planning, as we shall see in the next section.

Communication Planning

At the national level there are two types of communication planning which involve different aspects of communication development and planning processes. The first is "communication infrastructure planning," involving the development and maintenance of communication technology and facilities. The second is "communication operation planning," or the control and operation of communication elements and their contents.

In Singapore, there is no comprehensive communication planning either in infrastructure development or in the operation of the communication system. Whatever planning occurs is formulated within individual divisions or departments and processed through appropriate channels.

Communication infrastructure planning is usually short-term in nature and often subsumed under overall development planning. Agencies and departments responsible for given communication elements make their own plans for communication facilities and technology. Such plans are submitted by the ministry in charge either to the Finance Ministry as part of the annual budget requests, or as independent development projects to the ministerial Development Planning Committee, for deliberation and final approval. They are treated just like any other budget requests and development projects throughout the planning and decision-making procedures.

Several agencies can be identified for their respective responsibilities in communication infrastructure planning. The Telecommunication Authority of Singapore under the Ministry of Communication is probably the most important agency because of its responsibility for telephone, telegraph, and telex services, and the satellite communication network. Also under the Communication Ministry, the Postal Department is responsible for planning new post offices and other facilities for postal services. The Broadcasting Department under the Ministry of Culture formulates plans relating to the facilities for radio and television services. Under the Ministry of Education, the Singapore Educational Media Service (SEMS) prepares plans for the expansion and maintenance of its audio-visual media facilities for educational purposes. In addition to the above major agencies directly involved with communication infrastructure planning, activities involving minor communication planning elements can be identified in most departments and government offices.

The Ministry of Culture may be considered the key organization for overall policy in communication operation planning. The ministry is responsible for framing general guidelines for all major mass media so that their operations will be consistent with overall government communication policy (see chapter 5). The following units under the Ministry of Culture are especially relevant:

- Publicity Division: liaison with the *press,*
- Broadcasting Department: operation of *radio* and *television,*
- Board of Film Censors: censorship of *films* and film-related activities,
- The National Library: collection of all local *publications,*
- National Archives and Records Centre: storage of *records* of public and private institutions.

The Ministry of Culture is also responsible, as the licensing authority, for printing presses, publications and newspapers, and public entertainment.

For the operation of other communication systems, several other government agencies can also be identified:

- Telecommunication Authority of Singapore: operation of *telephone, telex,* and *telegraph* services, and the *satellite communication* network,

- Postal Department: operation of *postal* services,
- Singapore Educational Media Service: operation of *Educational Television* and other educational media services.

Although the general guidelines of communication policy are clear-cut and consistent, communication planning at the national level in Singapore is fragmentary. In order to understand the communication planning process better, analysis must be done at the institutional rather than the national level. In the following chapter, we will discuss the structure and operation of Radio Television Singapore (RTS) to illustrate communication planning at the institutional level in Singapore.

7

Communication Planning at the Institutional Level: Case Study of Radio Television Singapore

Communication planning, as defined by the Development Support Communication Services (DSCS) of the United Nations Development Program (UNDP), is essential for effective and efficient implementation of development projects (Rahim 1977, pp. 13-14). In Singapore, as was discussed in chapter 5, mass media are expected to play a major role to support, explicitly or implicitly, the objectives of nation-building. Among the mass media, radio and television have been put under direct and total control of the government; Radio Television Singapore (RTS) is "entrusted with the responsibility of interpreting the long-term objectives and policies of the Government, and particularly in maintaining a sense of national identity" (Ministry of Culture 1973).

In this chapter, we present a case study of RTS to illustrate communication planning at the institutional level in Singapore. Through the operation of RTS[5], we are able to see the conscious efforts made by the government to support, directly or indirectly, various development projects. The planning and implementation of policies are to be illustrated by RTS's selection, production, and scheduling of programs.

Organization and Operation

Radio service in Singapore started under private management in 1935, and was not included in government operations until the 1950s. In contrast, the question of the ownership and management of television was discussed before its introduction to Singapore in 1963. In 1956, the Committee Appointed to Examine the Possibility of Introducing Television in Singapore was established. In its final report (1957, p. 3), the committee suggested that television service should be offered "to the people of Singapore providing

[5]The survey is based on a quota sample of 612 Singaporeans aged 15 and over. The factors stratified in sampling are sex, ethnicity, working status and housing type. The detailed findings of the study are reported in Chen and Kuo (1978).

information, education, and entertainment, to the enrichment of individual life and fostering of national unity." Thus, from the very beginning, television was expected to offer information, education, and entertainment, in that order, for the benefit of the individual and the nation. The report of the committee proposed several conditions for the operation of the new television service:

1. Programs should be suited to local conditions and be such as to command a wide audience;
2. Proper standards of public morality and decency should be observed;
3. Service should not be subject to party political control, although there would always be an obligation on the Government of the day to ensure that general public interest would be safeguarded;
4. Standards of technical efficiency should be prescribed and maintained; and
5. The cost of service should not be such as to impose a heavy burden on the taxpayer. (1957, p. 3)

What is most interesting about the committee report is that it discussed three possible methods of operation: by a government department, by private commercial interest, and by a public corporation. Apparently with the BBC model in mind, the report recommended that television in Singapore should be run by a public corporation. The committee recommendations were not accepted in total. In 1963, the Broadcasting and Television Act was legislated, and television was introduced to Singapore under the administration of Radio Television Singapore as a department within the Ministry of Culture.

While any change in the organization and administration of the broadcasting service in Singapore is unlikely in the near future, the topic has not yet been totally closed. In 1969, the then acting Minister of Culture, Mr. Wee Toon Boon, announced in parliament: "It has been thought for quite some time that the public of Singapore will be better served by a statutory board, or even by a commercial corporation. The main advantage of a statutory board or of a commercial corporation, as opposed to a government department of radio and TV, is that such a structure leads to greater operational efficiency and convenience." He explained that it was possible to consider a structural change because the service had just become financially independent insofar as recurrent expenditure was concerned. And he added that "Whatever the outcome of that consideration, there is no reason to suggest that cultural and overall policy must be changed as a result of a change in structured organization" (*Straits Times,* April 11, 1969). The suggestion was apparently dropped.

Recently, the issue was brought up again in a letter to the editor that reads in part as follows:

> Perhaps it is time we thought seriously of turning our broadcasting division into a corporation along the lines

of the BBC and other government-financed broadcasting bodies around the world. (*Straits Times,* October 13, 1977)

At about the same time, a feature story in *Sunday Nation* showed convincingly that television and radio services in Singapore will not be able to survive financially without government support and funds (*Sunday Nation,* October 16, 1977).

By making television and radio broadcasting a part of government operation, the Singapore government exerts close control over the program contents of both media. Such an operation not only allows censorship of those programs considered undesirable to the interest of society, but makes it possible positively to plan and design programs to support development objectives sought by the government.

Radio Television Singapore is headed by a director, who is assisted by a deputy director and heads of divisions. There are five major divisions/units: News, Central Production Unit (CPU), Programmes, Commercial, and Engineering.

The News Division is an integrated unit with staff working for both radio and television. Radio Singapore broadcasts 46 news bulletins a day in the four official languages and six Chinese dialects (Hokkien, Teochew, Cantonese, Hainanese, Hakka, and Hokchew). Television Singapore produces 15-minute news bulletins in the evenings, in each of the official languages. A 15-minutes newsreel follows the news bulletins—five days per week in English, four days per week in Chinese, three days per week in Malay, and twice a week in Tamil. Television Singapore also telecasts a "news-in-brief" bulletin of three to five minutes duration in English in the evenings.

For news broadcasts, international news is taken from the wire services, and local news is covered by the department's own reporters and camera crews. The local news places heavy emphasis on government-related functions and activities. News broadcasts in different languages and dialects are basically the same, as is news released on both radio and television. Presently, there are two positions under the head of division in charge of producing news programs: "I Controller News" is responsible for the newscasts in English, Malay, and Tamil; "II Controller News" takes care of all Chinese newscasts and Chinese public affairs programs such as forums, debates, and so on. (Programs of public interest in English and other languages are the responsibility of the Central Production Unit.)

Newscasts on radio or television are informational in nature and serve the function of nation-building only indirectly through the selection of news. Typically, the achievements of ministries and speeches of government leaders are highlighted. The selection and presentation of international news also closely follows government policies in foreign affairs.

More direct support of development projects by the news division can be seen in the background "flashes" shown at the conclusion of each newscast. Usually, while the music ending the newscast is being played, a segment of film or a series of slides with a common theme are shown in support of the current national campaign. It might be a road safety campaign, a courtesy campaign, or any of the dozen campaigns being sponsored by the government every year.

RTS's Central Production Unit (CPU) plays a key role in development communication in both radio and television. It produces films, filmlets, slides, forums, talk shows and documentaries designed to provide analytic background on current affairs. According to a Ministry of Culture publication (1973), programs produced by the CPU "give the rationale for Government action, explain the aims of Government policy, and suggest to the audience a particular way or choice. Broad and national in scope, these programs are aimed at stimulating interest in the political, economic, and social developments of our society as well as those of other countries."

The CPU programs are generally development-conscious as well as informational and educational in nature, for example "Daily Digest" and "Quote for the Day" on radio, and "Opinion," "Debate," "Youth," and "Sports Desk" on television. Parliamentary proceedings are also reported in part on both radio and television. CPU programs usually relate to current affairs or issues. Again, topics and themes in different CPU programs are often chosen to create public awareness and to support certain public campaigns. However, topics of a more general nature, not specific to a given campaign, are also selected—themes such as modernization, pollution, and productivity.

The CPU is also responsible for the production of radio and television exchange programs, for exchange with member organizations of the Asian Broadcasting Union (ABU) and ASEAN countries. Some programs have been entered in overseas competitions with encouraging results.

The Programmes Division is responsible for both the production and the acquisition of programs from abroad for radio and television broadcasting. In the radio service, the Malay, Chinese, and Tamil sections produce and compile all their own programs. In the English radio section, imported programs constitute 10 percent of output.

The reliance on imported television programs is more obvious because of shortages of staff, funds, and suitable material. According to the Ministry of Culture, about one third of television programs are imported. These are mainly "canned" entertainment shows, series, and long films from the United States, the United Kingdom, Taiwan, and Hong Kong. Most of these imported programs are shows and films of high entertainment quality, in contrast to locally produced programs that are more informational and educational in nature. Imported programs are, therefore, extremely popular in Singapore. This situation has created some concern about external cultural influences and social implications in Singapore. Obviously, the imbalance between local versus imported programs, especially television, should be of concern to policymakers. The problem is probably common to most developing countries.

Due to the shortage of resources, reliance on foreign programs seems inevitable for RTS. The alternatives might be to reduce the number of transmission hours or to produce more local programs of lower quality. Neither is considered desirable, nor are they acceptable to the audience. Presently, RTS tries to exercise some control over imported programs by careful and stringent selection, as we shall discuss later.

RTS's Commercial Division runs an advertising service over both radio and television. There are two subsections under the division: the Commercial Radio Service, started in 1960, and the Commercial Television Service, started in 1964. Both services are in the four official languages of the Republic. Commercials in Chinese dialects were used previously but have been phased out since July 1, 1978, in support of the government's new emphasis on Mandarin in place of dialects.

RTS relies for only part of its financial revenues on commercials, which therefore have little influence on the contents and scheduling of programs. According to RTS Programme Code, "All scripts, spot advertisements and recorded programmes offered for the Commercial Service must be approved by the Broadcasting Department before broadcast." In addition, "the Broadcasting Department retains the right to cancel or postpone at any time any programme or period on the Commercial Service should this be considered necessary in the interests of the State or of the listening public." (See Appendix 3.) RTS can therefore adjust its programs and schedule with flexibility readily to serve the function of national development, such as when a speech by the prime minister is to be broadcast to the population.

As a rule, no commercials are permitted to interrupt educational and cultural programs. Similarly, no commercials are run throughout the news programs. "When it comes to documentaries . . . on art, music, historical serials, cultural shows and newscasts, ads are out" (*New Nation,* May 14, 1977). Although there have been constant complaints that Television Singapore is saturated with commercials, RTS claims that strict standing rules are followed to protect the viewers. The rules allow only one break for every half-hour show, two for a 45-minute show and three for a 60-minute show. The average number of commercials at each break is five, but may be increased to a maximum of eight for more popular shows, especially the Chinese serials. Each break lasts about four to five minutes. According to RTS, the commercials take up only about eight percent of total air time (*Straits Times,* April 19, 1978). Another report indicates that overall 35 to 40 percent of programs on Television Singapore do not have commercials. During prime time (from 7 to 10 p.m.) 30 percent of the shows are telecast without advertisements (*New Nation,* May 14, 1977).

Of all the divisions of RTS, the Engineering Division is the only one not directly involved with the design and production of programs. It provides technical support for both radio and television. Besides its day-to-day operational and maintenance commitments, the division is also responsible for overall hardware planning and development work.

Policy Decision Making and Planning

There are different levels of communication policy. At the most general and abstract level, the ethos of the political philosophy and the legal codes serve as general guidelines for the operation of RTS. At the more practical level, the cabinet is the highest decision-making machine that makes specific policy decisions that may directly or indirectly involve the work of RTS. Such decisions are conveyed to the Minister for Culture who communicates them to the director of broadcasting. They are then passed further down the bureaucratic hierarchy to section heads, controllers, and producers.

Within RTS, the director makes final decisions at the institutional level and is responsible for decision-making and planning. The director is assisted by a management committee which discusses and decides budget allocations, program changes, program placement, and other such issues. The committee is made up of the director of broadcasting, the chief engineer, the commercial manager, the controller for program administration, the controller for the central production unit, the two news controllers, the controller services, the head of the administrative section, the RTS chief accountant, and the senior executive engineer of the network (Malolos 1977, pp. 64, 66). However, for all practical purposes, overall program plans are made annually when the department makes its budget request to parliament, based on proposals made by section heads on their respective requests and estimates.

At a still lower level, the planning and production of a given program is the responsibility of the producer who has been assigned the job. The planning process goes the other way from low to high. Suggestions made by the producer or his staff must be discussed at the section head level and then sent up the hierarchy to the director for approval. However the producer is the main figure who is in charge of coordinating staff from other sections and making all necessary arrangements for a given program. In general, other than the producer (or assistant producer), staff involved may include a scriptwriter, a designer, a technical producer, the floor manager, an editor, and the studio crew. Careful planning and coordination are important throughout the process of production.

Program planning at RTS has to be done without sufficient feedback information from the audience. RTS relies mainly on the following sources to appraise the views of the audience:

1. TV program rating supplement issued once every six weeks by Survey Research Singapore, a commercial market research company. The report gives the ratings of programs over a six-week period and is prepared for commercial purposes. Ratings include only basic information on the size of audience for various programs, and do not provide information such as correlating popularity of a program with the characteristics of viewers (age, sex, ethnicity, occupation, etc.). It is obviously not comprehensive enough for program planning purposes.

2. There are letters and telephone calls from viewers or listeners, relating either to specific programs such as quizzes, competitions, and request programs, or to general programming or scheduling of RTS. The opinions and comments from this source vary greatly and are often contradictory. RTS records all suggestions and complaints received; the problem with such feedback is of course that these represent probably only the extreme views about RTS operation. The views of the "silent majority" are not tackled.
3. Still other information comes from the press, including letters to the editor and comments made by media critics or editors. RTS appears to be a favorite topic for readers who write to the newspapers, as such letters appear often, especially in *Straits Times.* Invariably, RTS makes an effort to reply to such letters, more to pacify those with complaints and to explain RTS policies, than to seek actively for suggestions for program planning. As a media critic puts it, "it is ironical that mass media [sic] has to rely on another mass medium, the Press, to maintain contact with viewers who write letters to the editor" (Koh 1973). Confronted with public comments and criticisms, the RTS as a government department may feel it necessary to protect its public image. Consequently,

> RTS policy-makers are hypersensitive to any criticism, as a result of which, policies are changing at a bewildering pace, so that producers, never quite sure what is allowed, stick to tried formulae. This sensitivity is attributable to the lack of a daily barometer to gauge audience reaction. (*Sunday Nation,* October 16, 1977)

The lack of effective evaluation of programs and audience responses is the theme of another critic:

> Up to now Television Singapore has yet to conduct a public survey to find out what are preferences of viewers. Beyond relying empirically on telephone calls and letters, it has made no attempt to find out what viewers want. Indeed, it has all along given viewers, in its opinion, what they ought to want. (Koh 1973)

Obviously, RTS planners and schedulers are aware of such information gaps. Public interest and demand for qualitative television programs were becoming quite apparent early in 1978. It was revealed in February 1978 that RTS will "conduct its first-ever audience survey for the purposes of programme planning and improving the quality of local and imported programmes" (*Straits Times,* February 22, 1978).

Program and Schedule Planning[6]

Radio Television Singapore takes great care in planning and scheduling programs in order to perform properly its role in nation-building and social development, while at the same time serving the population as a major source of entertainment. The planning process in RTS can most clearly be shown and appreciated from its efforts to obtain the following objectives:

1. To maintain a balance between programs of educational and informational nature (those directly development-oriented) and those of entertainment nature. Entertainment programs are also carefully chosen and scheduled.
2. To maintain a balance among the programs in the four official languages so that the contents of broadcasts can reach the linguistically diversified population.
3. To support national campaigns being promoted by government agencies or national organizations.

All of the above concerns require careful and conscious planning by RTS, and can best illustrate the planning of communication contents for specified objectives.

Development-Oriented Programs

Under government operation, radio and television broadcasting in Singapore is development-conscious and emphasizes information and education.

Newscasts produced by RTS's News Division serve the function of informing the audience. Programs produced by the Central Production Unit are concerned with current political and social issues and are both educational and informative in nature. These types of programs together with imported programs of cultural, educational, and scientific content are considered development-oriented. They are often placed on the prime-time schedule in order to attract a large audience. According to Mr. K.C. Lee, then acting Minister for Culture, "informative and educational programmes take up an average of nearly 35 percent of the total radio transmission hours and 30 percent of the total TV transmission hours" (*Straits Times,* November 12, 1975). He also reported to Parliament in 1975 that "nearly 60 percent of locally-produced programmes for TV are educational/informative," in contrast to about 54 percent in 1974. Such a percentage may be considered high in comparison with most of the developed and third world countries. It reflects an increase from earlier years, as the average weekly output of educational and informative programs was reported to be 22.9 percent in 1973, and 23.2 percent in early 1974. "TV Singapore is by far the largest user of documentaries in this region" (*Singapore Parliamentary Debates,* Vol. 33, 1974, Col. 516).

[6]A part of this section is discussed in Kuo 1977b and 1978.

Although imported TV entertainment programs are extremely popular, RTS has been very strict in selection and censorship to protect public taste and moral standards. A special committee in RTS must preview every film and videotape to be screened. According to a newspaper report, "more than 18,000 metres, or about 25 hours of TV film, were snipped off the air in 1975 by Radio Television Singapore censors on grounds of excessive violence. A number of crime series were also rejected for the same reason" (*New Nation,* February 22, 1977). In the same report, an RTS spokesman revealed that, "Generally, in getting programmes for telecast, a broad cross-section of the tastes, interests, sensitivities and values of our viewers is taken into account." Specifically, "scenes that are considered offensive in terms of violence are noted during preview and these are physically excised from films or, in the case of videotapes, these are edited out. If such eliminations impair continuity or presentation, the entire programme is rejected."

In 1976, RTS rejected en bloc, two highly-rated police and detective series comprising 52 one-hour episodes. Of individual episodes or series and feature films, 51 programs were banned under the category of "crime and violence." RTS rejects instances where "violence is perpetuated for no assignable reason or is distasteful, excessive, glorified or sensationalized to an extent warranting proscription" (*New Nation,* February 22, 1977). Some examples are:

- Protracted acts of brutality, a person being set upon—mugging, senseless brawling.
- Gory scenes of stabbing, strangulation.
- Repeated point-blank gunplay or acts of bombing, arson, and sabotage, especially with detailed close-ups.
- Rioting, lynching, and other similar mob-incited activities.

In practice, RTS has been able to restrict the number of police and detective programs to six per week, comprising an average of 4.8 percent of the station's weekly output. These programs are nevertheless among the most popular in Singapore.

Earlier in 1975 in a parliamentary discussion, it was revealed that 26 imported films had been banned from Television Singapore because of violent themes and detailed depiction of crime. For the same reason, 80 to 100 censorship cuts are made every year. "Apart from this stringent censorship, the number of police and detective dramas scheduled is regulated. Of the 225 programmes in a week, an average of only six such programmes are scheduled, and these are not telecast every day of the week. Programmes featuring law enforcement officers and crime investigators comprise only 5.7 percent of RTS output" (*Singapore Parliamentary Debates,* Vol. 34, 1975, Col. 704).

While violence on TV has been the concern both of the public and RTS itself, programs involving ambiguous moral standards are strictly banned. For instance, "Three's Company," an American series about two girls and a guy who share an apartment, was not acceptable because it was considered too permissive by local standards.

Another aspect of communication planning by RTS involves the scheduling of programs. In both radio and television programs, the schedule invariably takes into consideration the nature of the program and the type of target audience it appeals to (in terms of ethnicity, language, sex, and occupation). Programs targeted for housewives and students are scheduled at proper slots different from those for family viewing and for the general public. Newscasts on television are given prime time in the evening to attract a wider audience. Children's programs are typically scheduled earlier in the evening between 5 and 7 p.m. Recently it has been suggested that action-packed shows should be shifted to late-night slots. On radio, programs in Chinese dialects that appeal to the older generation are slotted at later hours.

Since four radio stations generally broadcast in four languages and cater to audiences of different linguistic backgrounds, not much conflict or competition is perceived between them. For television, the situation is different. The two TV channels compete not only with each other, but with two channels of Television Malaysia, which get perfect reception in Singapore, and may exert some influence on schedule planning processes.

Communication Policy of Multilingualism

It is significant that the maxim of RTS is "From Many Cultures, One Voice," reflecting the multicultural and multilingual nature of its programs and audience. To support the government policy of multilingualism, which prescribes that all four official languages should be treated equally, RTS makes its programs available in all four languages.

Since four channels are provided—one for each language group, the distribution of radio transmission hours in the four languages is relatively equal, as shown in Table 30.

Table 30

Language and RTS Broadcasting in Singapore, 1975

	Language of Program				
	Malay	**Chinese***	**Tamil**	**English**	**Total**
Radio Singapore					
Hours Per Week	126	147	105	126	504
Percent	25.0	29.2	20.8	25.0	100.0
Television Singapore					
Minutes Per Week	685	1,560	560	3,435	6,240
Percent	11.0	25.0	9.0	55.0	100.0

Source: Based on *Parliament Debate Report*, Notice Paper No. 80 of 1975; also *Straits Times*, November 12, 1975.

*Including Mandarin and six other Chinese dialects.

Official government policy sets the ratio of different language television program hours at 20 percent Malay, 35 percent Chinese, 10 percent Tamil, and 35 percent English (*Singapore Parliamentary Debates,* Vol. 28, 1968-69, Col. 583). Actual operation however shows some deviation from the above goal, as shown in Table 30. The higher proportion of transmission hours in English is due partly to the more ready availability of imported programs in that language—the same can be said of Mandarin programs—and partly to the dominant status of English in Singapore as the official working language.

In order to maintain a more balanced linguistic distribution of programs, RTS provides subtitling. On principle, non-English programs are supplied with English subtitles. However, English programs are more often provided with Malay subtitles to compensate for the shortage of Malay-language programs. As a result, usually, up to three languages, in either oral or written form, are available at any one time between the two channels of Television Singapore. In recent years, Television Singapore has begun to dub popular English-language documentaries in Mandarin, Malay, and Tamil to make up for the lack of similar programs in those languages.

Since RTS is entrusted with the role of nation-building and since the basic rationale of multilingualism is to provide information to a population of diversified language background, it is relevant to look at the proportion of information/education programs offered in each language. Based on statistics from the Ministry of Culture, we find that informational and educational programs take up an average of about 34 percent of total radio transmission hours and 29 percent of total television hours (see Table 31). It is especially interesting to note that the percentages of information and education program hours within various language transmissions are higher in the three ethnic languages than in English. In Tamil and Malay television programs in particular, the relatively shorter periods of transmission are slightly compensated by higher proportions of information and education programs. It seems that the Tamil and Malay language audiences can be expected to turn to other language channels, notably English, for entertainment. But ethnic language programs of an informational and educational nature are maintained to make sure that messages are disseminated to members of the various ethnic communities.

Table 31

Percentage of Information and Education Programs* in Singapore, by Language, 1975

	Malay	Chinese†	Tamil	English	Total
Radio Singapore	33.3	38.8	36.2	27.8	34.1
Television Singapore	39.4	27.2	46.4	24.9	29.0

Source: Based on *Parliament Debate Report*, Notice Paper No. 80 of 1975; also *Straits Times*, November 12, 1975.

*As defined and calculated by the Ministry of Culture, Singapore.
†Including Mandarin and six other Chinese dialects.

The most popular TV programs in Singapore are the entertaining ones in Chinese and English. A report of television program ratings in late 1976 reveals that all except two of the ten most popular programs were in Chinese and most were produced in either Taiwan or Hong Kong. Interestingly, many television serialized dramas in Mandarin, imported from Taiwan, seem to attract a multilingual and multiethnic audience. Such popular Chinese dramatic series are mainly quasi-historical stories or contemporary romances and have frequently been the target of criticism by local Chinese newspapers. Some of them are nevertheless highly popular, an example being the Taiwan-produced series "Justice Pao," in 1976. According to a (non-Chinese) MP in a parliamentary discussion,

> This popularity of "Justice Pao" with a multilingual audience shows that a programme with a cultural flavour of one of the main cultural streams of our society can . . . have an audience transcending a particular ethnic group. (*Singapore Parliamentary Debates,* Vol. 35, 1976, Col. 627)

Television is a popular medium of entertainment in Singapore. Yet different programs in different languages attract different types of audiences. The phenomenon has a special meaning in Singapore because of its unique sociolinguistic complexity. The older generation tends to be more interested in programs in ethnic languages and Chinese dialects, while the youngsters are more likely to be English-educated and appreciative of modern Western culture as reflected in the imported television programs. As a result, a reader wrote to the editor of *Straits Times,* "there is at least one unhappy person in a family every night" (May 14, 1977). Although the basic choice is between only two television channels (not counting Television Malaysia channels which have only limited followers in Singapore), differences in taste and linguistic preference among family members may result in conflict over the selection of programs. Therefore, there have been requests to either cut down a certain type of program or rearrange the schedule to avoid the clash of two highly popular dramas at the same time. One youngster sought sympathy as a loser in the family drama of who-gets-to-watch-what by saying,

> We of the younger generation who prefer the modern-day programmes have to give way to our elders who cannot bear to miss a minute of their drama serial. (*Straits Times,* May 14, 1977)

There does not seem to be any easy way to solve the problem which involves decision making in the family. As an RTS spokesman put it, "We can't please everybody, you know" (*Straits Times*, May 18, 1977).

Other than planning to have equitable proportions of programs in various official languages, RTS also supports the language policy of the government through other means. One example is the introduction of programs making use of two languages—English and Mandarin. Programs such as "Youth" and "Student Concert" tend to attract a number of the emergent bilingual population and reflect a genuine effort on the part of RTS to support the bilingual policy, although bilingualism in this context seems to mean only English and Mandarin, the two dominant languages in Singapore.

Radio Singapore also regularly broadcasts various language courses, serving more directly the function of language teaching. (Educational programs for primary and secondary students are provided on television by Singapore Educational Media Service under the supervision of the Ministry of Education. RTS is responsible for the transmission of those programs.)

More recently, to support the prime minister's appeal to encourage the use of Mandarin in place of Chinese dialects, RTS has, since July 1, 1978, been phasing out radio and television commercials in Chinese dialects. It has been suggested that programs in Chinese dialects, including some very popular serialized Cantonese dramas from Hong Kong, will be dubbed in Mandarin. Since 1976, operas in Chinese dialects are shown only at Chinese New Year season. However, dialect programs in both radio and television still attract an audience from the older generation, as quite often they are the only source of information and entertainment for this segment of the population. In the process of phasing out Chinese-dialect programs, the RTS, therefore, has to be sensitive to this group and accommodate their needs as much as possible.

Support of National Campaigns

Radio and television broadcasting, like other components of the national communication network, provide constant support of various public campaigns being promoted almost perennially in Singapore. Most direct support comes from programs produced by the Central Production Unit, such as forums, panel discussions, and documentaries, for the purposes of creating public awareness and advocating messages.

A more subtle form of support comes from news coverage. Activities relating to current campaigns such as the opening ceremony of a certain exhibit and speeches by government leaders, are given significant coverage in the newscasts. Flashes and slides are shown at the end of each newscast reinforcing the theme of an ongoing campaign.

Campaign messages appear as advertising items just like other commercials on television and radio. Such commercials are treated like other commercials in terms of advertising rates, except that they are accepted on very short notice and may be given preferential treatment in the allotment of time. In the courtesy campaign in 1978, for instance, when the campaign was started in April, a two-minute courtesy jingle in English, Mandarin, and Malay was broadcast over radio at breakfast time between 6 and 9 a.m. On television, a color slide with a bright, cheery, smiling face and bearing the courtesy slogan in English and Chinese was flashed on the screen for seven seconds before such popular drama programs as "Future Cop," "Bionic Woman," and "Switch." A filmlet of five minutes was produced by Cepta TV and the Singapore Tourist Promotion Board for showing both on television and in local cinemas for the same purpose (*Straits Times,* April 5, 1978).

In most cases, campaign messages can easily be included in the existing programs for a particular target audience. For instance, during the campaign to promote frozen fish so as to reduce the price of fresh fish, recipes using frozen fish were included in family and women's magazine shows. Similarly, quizzes and children's shows can easily have questions and stories regarding road safety inserted at the time of a road safety campaign.

Sometimes a new program may be introduced to promote campaign messages on a more lasting basis. Thus, a "Telemetric" series was put on in 1977 as a novel way to encourage Singaporeans to use and understand the metric system. Similarly, when the Ministry of Defense wanted to encourage people to join the armed services, a new program, "Armed Forces Hour," was started on radio.

When issues of national interest require national attention, priority is readily granted by RTS for special programs. For instance, press conferences or interviews with political detainees have been telecast as an accepted means of "public confessions" for years in Singapore. Similarly, press conferences given by the prime minister during his foreign visits may also be shown to the local audience. In early 1978, the prime minister himself appeared twice on television, once using the English language and the second time using Mandarin, with a group of panelists to answer questions on the problem of bilingualism in Singapore. All these are examples of using television "to take the whole nation into a collective tutorial on the problems of politics" (Thomson 1974, p. 25).

Evaluation of RTS Planning

The problem that most, if not all, radio and television stations in developing countries face is where to draw the line between serving the needs of the country and satisfying the demands of viewers and listeners. Translated into the language of program planning, this is the problem of maintaining a proper balance between information/education programs and entertainment. The underlying conflict is that, while the government leaders may want the population to be exposed to more development-oriented communication messages, the audience sees radio and television basically as media of entertainment, as our survey results have shown.

In Singapore, radio and television are operated by the government, their main functions being to inform, educate, and entertain, with emphasis on the first two. Unlike commercial networks in other countries, they do not have the objective of making money to survive financially. But unlike public service broadcasting stations in other countries, they do put out commercials throughout the day. Government backing for programs means that the RTS is free from the influence of advertising agencies and large corporations in deciding the kind of programs to be broadcast and telecast; there is no need to please the large majority of the audience with programs of superficial or frivolous content. The station can therefore transmit more serious programs such as documentaries and forums even though these are costly to produce and are telecast without commercial sponsorship.

As a government operation, radio and television in Singapore have not been used effectively as platforms for debate on sensitive issues, although recently there seems to have been some attempt to encourage more discussion of controversial issues on these media. Significant changes in that direction may take a long time.

The need to cater to a multicultural population of different linguistic preferences has proved costly. Local and foreign productions have to be carefully vetted for innuendos that might upset the stability of the nation by insulting one group. The need to broadcast in four different languages means that energies have to be channeled in four directions. Time, money, equipment, and staff have to be quadruplicated. Shows have to be subtitled, films cut to suit producers in the different language sections and programs dubbed in different languages. The apparently manifold channels and programs actually leave the audience and readers with a narrow choice of content. As far as development-oriented communication contents are concerned, the wide range of choice and the abundance of contents are more apparent than real. It should however be emphasized that such redundancy is desirable and necessary (see Rogers 1976, p. 235), since quite a proportion of the population is still monolingual and can only be reached in one language/dialect.

Financially, RTS does not seem to receive sufficient funding from the government. The main estimate (excluding hardware and physical development expenditures) for the Broadcasting Department in fiscal year 1976 was $23.15 million. This was marginally improved to $24.93 million in 1977 and $26.16 million in 1978. The tight budget makes it difficult for RTS to recruit qualified staff and artists for its programs. Furthermore, RTS has been suffering from "brain drain" as some of its staff have found it financially more rewarding to work in commercial settings. As civil servants, RTS staff are not paid overtime, nor are they paid any kind of shift allowance. Most part-timers, weather announcers, news-readers, singers, or actors and actresses are also poorly paid and thus continue to perform out of interest rather than for money. A newspaper report reveals that in 1978 the RTS budget for a 10-minute production was $1,200 and for a 45-minute production, $1,800. This was far below Hong Kong television companies which allotted four times the sum for each class (*Straits Times,* April 17, 1978). Another report reveals that,

> In Hong Kong, for example, the musical variety show "Enjoy Yourself Tonight" has a minimum production budget of $15,000 per programme. In Singapore, a similar show, "Musical Showcase," which is also one of the most popular locally-produced programmes, is allotted only $1,500. This makes it extremely difficult for the producer to hire top artistes (*Sunday Nation*, October 16, 1977).

While RTS has for some time been the target of criticism regarding the quality of its programs, it is only fair to note the financial and structural constraints that shape its output.

8

Communication Planning at the Project Level: Case Study of Family Planning Communication

In Singapore, as in other developing countries, the communication network and resources are used constantly to support a set of well-defined development objectives. This has been referred to as "project level communication planning," whereby "communication planning is carried out as a support to the substantive project planning" (Rahim 1978, p. 9). Such projects may be carried out for relatively short periods and still receive intensive and comprehensive coverage, examples being various national campaigns carried out perennially in Singapore. Working committees are often organized on an ad hoc basis to mobilize and coordinate efforts to fight for a social cause or to promote new attitudes or behavior patterns defined as desirable. These campaigns invariably involve intensive use of communication resources (Wee 1977).

At times, however, the development issue involved may be such that continuous efforts are called for over a long period of time to attain the set of development goals. In such cases, a permanent agency entrusted with specific functions is formed as part of the government structure. If the nature of the project requires extensive use of communication resources (for example, the literacy drive, health programs, extension education, or family planning and birth control), communication planning is carried out as part of overall project planning.

We will now discuss the family planning communication program as part of the operation of the Singapore Family Planning and Population Board (SFPPB) as an example of project level communication planning in Singapore. SFPPB's communication programs include both regular IEC (information, education, and communication) activities and intensive family planning campaigns of short duration. The programs make use of almost all communication resources available and are supported by the existing organizational structure in the society. Our analysis will therefore illustrate not only the use of the communication system but also the participation of the total societal system to achieve a set of well-defined project goals.

Family Planning in Singapore

Organized family planning efforts in Singapore began in 1949 with the formation of the Singapore Family Planning Association (SFPA). Although promotion of family planning was initiated primarily out of concern for the health and welfare of mothers and children, in later years, population control became the primary objective. In 1959, the government of Singapore adopted an official national policy in favor of family planning. With the establishment of the Singapore Family Planning and Population Board (SFPPB) in 1966, the government assumed all responsibility for family planning on a national scale. The Board is responsible for directing and coordinating all family planning activities in the republic.

Confronted with a rapidly growing population on a densely populated island, the SFPPB launched its first Five-Year National Family Planning Program from 1966 to 1970 and its second Five-Year Program from 1970 to 1975, with successful results in both periods.

The First Five-Year Plan (1966-1970)

The program was aimed at providing good clinic services, on the assumption that there was enough awareness as well as sufficient motivation for women to accept family planning, if the necessary clinic facilities were made available. The goal was to provide services for 60 percent of all married women aged 15-44 years within five years, with the assumption that the remaining 40 percent were either practicing family planning with private practitioners or did not require services at all. The main target for the first Five-Year Plan was to reduce the Crude Birth Rate (CBR) of 32 per thousand in 1964 to around 20 per thousand by 1970.

At the end of the first five years, the clinical records showed that a total of 156,556 women had accepted family planning. This was about 60 percent of all married women aged 15-44 years. The CBR was brought down to 22.1 per thousand in 1970—only slightly short of the target. The first Five-Year Plan was, therefore, considered successful.

The Board recognized from the beginning that providing services alone would be inadequate for promoting the practice of family planning. The Information and Education Committee, which included representatives from the Ministry of Culture and its Broadcasting Department (Radio Television Singapore), was set up in July 1966, to help the Board achieve its objectives through communication with the public.

The publicity was geared toward generating an awareness of family planning and population control, and creating an atmosphere conducive to practicing family planning. The theme of an island-wide campaign in 1967 was "Plan Your Family Small." After trying to reach the general public the communicators turned to specific groups of individuals who needed to be persuaded to practice family planning. All postpartum women in government maternity hospitals were encouraged and given appointments to attend maternal and health family planning clinics one month after their delivery. Newlyweds were invited to attend marriage guidance talks given in various languages.

Another campaign in 1970 had a more optimistic theme: "Plan for a Small and Happy Family." Posters were displayed to propagate the advantages of a small family: "Small Families have More to Eat," "Small Families have More to Spend," "Small Families have Better Health," "Small Families Own More," and so on. The 1970 program saw a continuation of the activities of the previous years. Besides the usual mass media messages, the Board initiated activities in community centers and among other groups, including talks, lectures, exhibitions, and demonstrations.

The Second Five-Year Plan (1971-1975)

The next part of the program was aimed at consolidating the efforts of the first five years with an annual recruitment of 16,000 new acceptors to achieve a total of 80,000 new registrants with the Board by the end of the period. The Board soon realized that large numbers of men and women from the postwar "baby boom" were then entering the reproductive group and having their own babies. The other "problem" group was the "hard-core" women who belonged to the high parity, older age groups, mostly of lower educational and socioeconomic status. The average expectation of family size was 3.6 children, but because of the preference for male children, the completed family size actually averaged 4.3 children.

In light of this major problem, the information/communication program of the Board modified its directions from 1972–1973 onward. This change in directions is summarized as (SFPPB Paper No. 34, 1975, p.9):

1. Intensive and extensive educational/informational/publicity activities to promote the two-child norm (and to reduce sex preference for sons) particularly among the large number of young men and women entering the reproductive age group.
2. Promotion of sterilization among couples with two or more children as well as further liberalization of the Abortion Law to complement the contraceptive program implemented through family planning clinics.
3. Upgrading the quality of family planning clinical services to ensure that couples practice continuous effective contraception.
4. Introduction and intensification of various incentive/disincentive measures aimed at the promotion of the small family norm.
5. Greater emphasis on research and evaluation studies to provide a scientific feedback system on which to base program decisions.
6. Training of the staff to upgrade their technical knowledge and motivational skills.

These priorities led to a massive family planning educational and publicity campaign in 1972. The necessity for continued publicity led to the establishment of the Information, Education, and Communication Unit (IEC Unit) in October 1972, to ensure that family planning education, information, and communication activities could be maintained and carried out on a continuous year-round basis, instead of being confined to campaign periods only. The Board continued to use mass media communication, interpersonal communication, exhibitions, demonstrations, seminars, and so on to promote the program throughout the second Five-Year Plan and thereafter.

The goal set for the second Five-Year Plan was to reduce the CBR from 22.1 per thousand in 1970 to 18.0 per thousand by 1975. As it happened, the CBR was reduced to 17.8 in 1975; the total fertility rate fell to 2.104, and the Net Reproduction Rate to 0.978. The target set for the plan was therefore reached.

The long-term goal of SFPPB is to achieve Zero Population Growth (ZPG) as soon as possible, by maintaining the replacement level. Since replacement level fertility was achieved in 1975, it is estimated that the long-term objective of ZPG will be reached in Singapore around the year 2030.

SFPPB Organization and Decision Making

The Singapore Family Planning and Population Board consists of 15 members chaired by the Deputy Director of Medical Services (Health). The other members are representatives of maternal and child health services, government hospitals, the Department of Statistics, the Social Welfare Department, the University of Singapore, the Ministry of Culture, the Institute of Education, and private obstetricians and gynecologists. The function of the Board is to decide general policy matters and formulate future plans and projects of the national family planning and population program.

Under the Board, five committees assist in the implementation of general policy—namely, Executive; Information, Education, and Communication; Medical; Research and Evaluation; and Training.

Assisting the chairman and second in the hierarchy is the executive secretary in charge of the different functional units of the Board. Another assistant to the chairman is the senior health officer who is responsible for the maternal and child health services of the Board. Projects of the Board are implemented by the five functional Technical Units (see Chart 1):

1. Clinical Services Unit;
2. Cytology Unit;
3. Information, Education, and Communication (IEC) Unit;
4. Research and Evaluation Unit;
5. Training Unit.

In addition, the Administrative Services Unit serves as the central coordinating body.

Leadership in the SFPPB rests with the chairman of the Board, the executive committee, the executive secretary, the senior health officer and the five unit heads. The chairman and the Board members meet quarterly to

Chart 1

Singapore Family Planning and Population Board Organization Chart

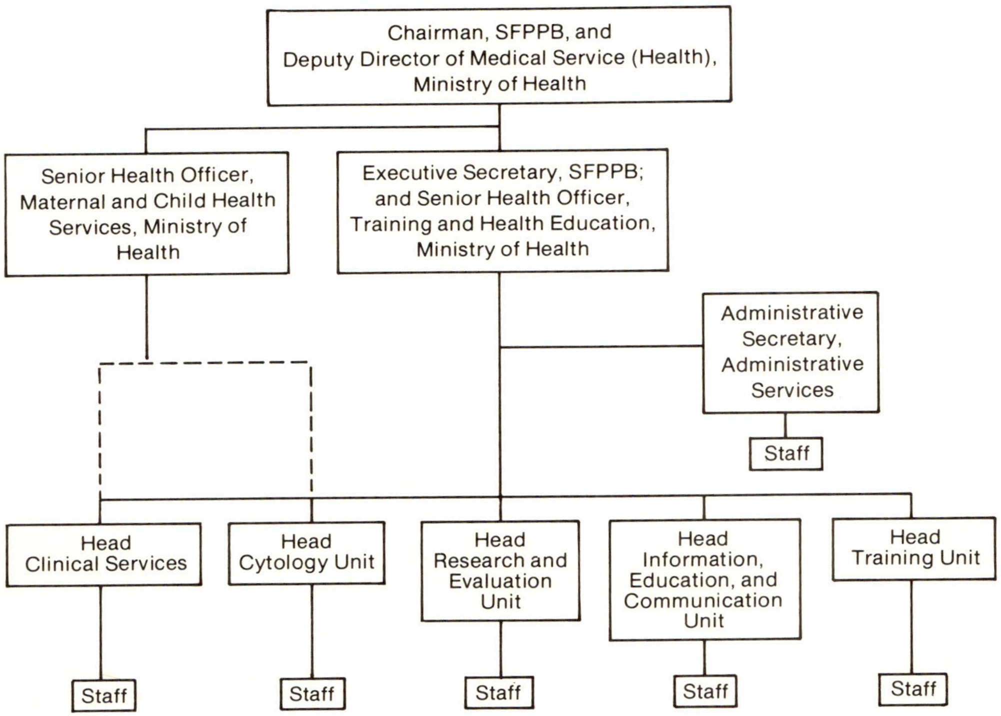

Source: Singapore Family Planning and Population Board, 1975a, p. 59.

decide general policy, approve the budget, and discuss future plans and projects.

In a study of the administration of the SFPPB from 1966 to 1973, John (1976) pointed out that leadership was composed entirely of medical doctors, many of them women. This suggests that family planning in Singapore is perceived primarily as a medical function with emphasis on clinical services. Doctors provide advice on the use of contraceptives and can handle abortion and sterilization cases effectively. However, such an administrative structure negates Rogers' notion that family planning programs would be more successful if controlled by qualified administrators rather than medical doctors (Rogers 1973, p. 327). According to John (1976, pp. 56-57), the medical administrators in SFPPB have received special professional training in management and administration conducted by the government, and have been able to perform the dual functions of administration and provision of services satisfactorily.

Because of the close relationship between the Board and various government agencies, and the strong and extensive support for the family planning program by the top-ranking political leaders, it is likely that the decision-making process in the SFPPB may involve participation from external sources.

Within the Board, the functional heads exercise power within their own units and are responsible for activities and personnel in their departments. According to John (1976, p. 57), there appears to be close coordination between low-level personnel and heads of units, and between the heads and the executive committee. Meetings held at regular intervals include the chairman, the senior health officer, the executive secretary, and the functional heads, so permitting the various functions to be implemented efficiently. John points out that the organizational system of the SFPPB shows the following characteristics:

1. Superiors are supportive of subordinates and have high performance goals for the organization;
2. There is a high level of communication both upwards and downwards within the organization;
3. There is a high degree of cooperation within and among work groups in the organization; and
4. Overall, this produces an organization marked by a sufficiently high degree of participation of all members at all levels in the work of the organization. (John 1976, p. 58)

Interorganizational Ties

Since its inception in 1966, the SFPPB has sought assistance and cooperation from other government and nongovernment agencies to carry out its missions successfully. The Board provides contraceptives and male sterilization services through its own clinics, but female sterilizations and abortions are carried out in the Ministry of Health institutions over which the Board has no direct administrative jurisdiction. The communication programs, though largely carried out by the Board, also require assistance from the Ministry of Culture, particularly its Broadcasting Division, the schools under the jurisdiction of the Ministry of Education, the People's Association, labor unions, and the press.

There does not seem to be any formal coordinating mechanism for population policies, although the senior officials of some government organizations, for example, the director of broadcasting and some senior officials of the Ministry of Health, serve as ex-officio members of the Board. However, according to Wan and Loh (forthcoming), an informal coordinating system was set up in 1972-73 when the Board established liaison with various government ministries, statutory bodies and private organizations, each of which has designated a liaison officer. The system was established mainly for information, education, and communication purposes, rather than to incorporate population or demographic considerations in the sectoral programs of those organizations.

Wan and Loh (forthcoming) further point out that the most powerful mechanism for coordination "seems to be the acute consciousness amongst senior civil servants in all government ministries and statutory boards of government policies in general, including those policies not directly relevant to their own Ministries or work programmes."

> Thus in implementing programmes of his own sector, the senior civil servant is continuously conscious of any adverse effects of his measures on other sectoral programmes and he is alert to ways in which his programmes may support or reinforce government policies in other areas. This pervasive consciousness of government policies from the top political level down to various levels of the civil service is the most important element for coordinated action. (Wan and Loh, forthcoming)

The interorganizational ties between the SFPPB and Radio Television Singapore (RTS) demonstrate the relationship and support involved.

As a rule, RTS generally supports family planning programs by reporting related activities such as exhibits, seminars, and speeches in its newscasts. The theme of family planning is often incorporated in the contents of programs relating to women, youth, and children. This type of support is often initiated by RTS which perceives family planning as part of national policy and in the interest of the public.

The relationship between the SFPPB and the commercial section of RTS is more formal. The SFPPB is treated like any other organization and charged the same rates for commercial exposure time. However, Television

Singapore does waive its rules slightly at times by giving preferred positions for exposure paid at (lower) rotational rates. Furthermore, although it is the normal practice of RTS to allow a month between the contract and eventual exposure, national family planning campaign requests would be accepted as little as four or five days before the first exposure. The Board's relationships with other government or quasi-government organizations are very much characterized by the same "soft formalism" as those with Television Singapore.

In carrying out SFPPB's communication program, the IEC unit often seeks help from other government organizations such as the People's Association, the Ministry of Education, and the Ministry of Culture. Many educational and publicity activities are carried out at community centers. Two large-scale seminars for community leaders have been organized annually for several years, and talks are held frequently at the community centers. Liaison with trade union leaders and employers has resulted in family planning and population matters being incorporated into trade union leaders'/workers' education programs. Since 1973–1974, the Ministry of Education has introduced population education into the curriculum for primary school students and is planning its inclusion in the syllabus for secondary schools. Teachers involved in family planning and population education are attending seminars organized by the SFPPB (Wan and Loh, forthcoming).

Strategies of Family Planning Communication

The SFPPB has been aware of the importance of family planning communication from the very beginning of its national program in 1966. Communication aspects of the program have been increasingly emphasized over the years, leading to the establishment of the Information, Education and Communication (IEC) Unit in 1972 as one of the five technical units of the Board.

The IEC Unit plans and implements all family planning education and publicity. The head of the Unit is assisted by a medical officer and followed in the hierarchy by communication officers, nursing officers, and health education officers. Within the SFPPB organization, there are also communication officers in the Training Unit, but the degree of coordination between communication officers in the two units is not known. However, from the hierarchical structure of both units, it appears that communication policies are not initiated by low-level communication officers but by top-level personnel (see John 1976, p. 50).

In the early phase of the communication program, the strategy initiated by the Board was to generate public awareness through the mass media and bring the subject of family planning into the open. Although over the years intense publicity was carried out over the mass media, it was soon realized that the media can do no more than generate awareness and publicize the availability of services. To give an individual real motivation to accept the concept and to practice family planning, strategies of interpersonal persuasive communication through the influence of community leaders and health agents have also been adopted. The IEC program of the SFPPB therefore consists of a wide variety of activities conducted throughout the year through almost every channel of communication available.

In this section, we discuss the use of different means of communication as part of the program in Singapore to propagate the messages of family planning. The following communication categories are to be analyzed:

1. Mass Media Communication, including printed media (newspapers, pamphlets, brochures), broadcasting media (television, radio, Rediffusion), and cinemas;
2. Group Communication, including exhibitions, public meetings, and public talks and discussions;
3. Interpersonal Communication, including visits with health agents, community leaders, and telephone information service;
4. Other Promotional Media, including the use of posters, street banners, bus panels, car stickers, postal marks, and novelty items like ball-point pens, key chains, shopping bags, and so forth.

Mass Media Communication

Printed Media

As discussed above, newspapers in Singapore are generally very supportive of government developmental projects, and frequently carry news articles, press releases, and feature stories about family planning, and give advance notice of events such as public speeches and exhibits connected with family planning. The Chinese press in particular often publish, as sort of a welfare service, stories of large families running into financial difficulties, thus indirectly supportive of small family norms. During the campaign period, when intensive promotional activities were being carried out, newspapers often printed editorial comments in support.

More directly, the SFPPB also makes use of newspaper advertisements to publicize its messages. In 1974 and 1975, when the Board carried out campaigns to publicize its Telephone Information Service (TIS) (see below), a total sum of $22,209 was spent for advertisements in six local newspapers, both to promote the small family norm and to publicize the TIS's telephone number. The period of advertising and the total number of insertions are shown in Table 32.

Other types of printed media used include pamphlets, brochures, and handbooks. These are high content materials which appeal to the literate population. At certain seminars or public talks attended by opinion and community leaders, handbooks are often prepared and distributed. They may therefore be used by such leaders for further dissemination or to help them organize discussion groups for the same purpose. Pamphlets and brochures are distributed during talks and public meetings and at family planning clinics.

Table 32

SFPPB Advertising through Newspapers in the 1975 TIS Campaign

Newspaper	Days of Advertising	Period of Advertising	Total Insertions	Total Cost (S$)
Nanyang Siang Pau	Monday, Wednesday, Friday	Dec. 30, 1974-May 26, 1975	63	4,536
Sin Chew Jit Poh	Tuesday, Thursday, Saturday	Dec. 31, 1974-May 29, 1975	63	5,103
New Nation	Tuesday, Friday	Dec. 31, 1974-May 23, 1975	42	2,364
Straits Times	Monday, Wednesday	Jan. 1, 1975-May 28, 1975	42	5,796
The Sunday Times	Sunday	Jan. 5, 1975-May 25, 1975	21	3,150
Berita Harian	Thursday, Saturday	Jan. 2, 1975-May 24, 1975	42	1,260
Total			273	22,209

Source: L. Lee 1976, p. 34.

Broadcasting Media

As discussed earlier, Radio Television Singapore often takes the initiative in supporting SFPPB programs, in much the same way as do the newspapers. Programs with contents related to family planning are specially produced during intensive campaigns. For instance, during the 1972 campaign, Television Singapore arranged and televised several 10-minute forums on family planning in each of the four official languages. There was also a public forum on sterilization, where four experts in the fields of family and population planning spoke.

More directly, the SFPPB makes use of RTS's commercial service to put on slogans, spot announcements, filmlets/slides, and flashes over radio and television at regular intervals. The following spot announcements are examples of such messages during the TIS campaign in 1974 and 1975 (L. Lee 1976, p. 31):

> (Male Voice): "Family life is more pleasant when fears are absent. Remove fears of unwanted pregnancies with Sterilization—the most effective and safe method for family limitation. Ring 538766."
>
> (Female Voice): "In Singapore, three out of every ten women use the contraceptive pill and they are happy because they will not have unwanted children. You can join them. Ring 538766."

The schedule and the total number of announcements for these campaigns during March-June 1974, and January-March 1975 are shown in Tables 33 and 34.

Cinemas

Slides and filmlets on family planning are shown in cinemas in Singapore before feature films. In the 1975 TIS campaign, such slides, prepared in different languages for different types of audience, were shown in 49 cinemas in Singapore, with a total of 1,299 cinema shows costing $6,765 during the three-month campaign.

Group Communication

Exhibitions

Exhibitions have been used frequently since the beginning of the national family planning program in Singapore, with the first one held at the end of 1966 and visited by nearly 100,000 people. In January 1967, the second family planning exhibition was held and about 72,000 attended.

Table 33

SFPPB Advertising through Broadcasting Media in the 1974 TIS Campaigns

Medium	Language	Announcements per Week	Duration (weeks)	Period	Total Spot Announcements
TV	English	6	8	Mar. 18-May 12, 1974	48
		3	4	May 13-June 9, 1974	12
	Chinese	6	8	Mar. 18-May 12, 1974	48
		3	4	May 13-June 9, 1974	12
	Malay	2	8	Mar. 18-May 12, 1974	16
		1	4	May 13-June 9, 1974	4
	Tamil	2	8	Mar. 18-May 12, 1974	16
		1	4	May 13-June 9, 1974	4
Subtotal					160
Radio	English	8 or 10 on alternate weeks	12	Mar. 18-June 9, 1974	102
	Chinese	9 or 10 on alternate weeks	12	Mar. 18-June 9, 1974	116
	Malay	4	12	Mar. 18-June 9, 1974	48
	Tamil	3	12	Mar. 18-June 9, 1974	36
Subtotal					302
Redif-difusion	English	21	2	Mar. 18-Apr. 30, 1974	42
		14	18	May 1-Aug. 4, 1974	252
	Chinese	28	4	Mar. 18-Apr. 14, 1974	112
		14	16	Apr. 15-Aug. 4, 1974	224
Subtotal					630
Total					1,092

Source: L. Lee 1976, p. 32.

Table 34

SFPPB Advertising through Broadcasting Media in the 1975 TIS Campaigns

Medium	Language/Type of Advertisement	Announcements per Week	Frequency Spots/Day x	Days/Week	Period	Total Spot Announcements
Television	English/slide	6	2	3	Jan. 8-Feb. 15, 1975	36
	/filmlet	3	1	3	Jan. 8-Mar. 4, 1975	24
	/slide	9	3	3	Feb. 20-Mar. 14, 1975	26
	Chinese	9	3	3	Jan. 10-Mar. 18, 1975	54
		3	3	3	Mar. 10-Mar. 13, 1975	6
	Malay	3	1	3	Jan. 8-Feb. 16, 1975	24
					Feb. 24-Mar. 16, 1975	22
	Tamil	2	1	2	Jan. 9-Feb. 14, 1975	12
					Feb. 20-Mar. 14, 1975	8
Total		35				212
Radio	English					
	/Daytime B	7	1	7	Jan. 7-Mar. 7, 1975	73
	/Breakfast	14	2	7	Jan. 7-Mar. 7, 1975	104
		4	1	4	Mar. 8-Mar. 11, 1975	4
	Chinese*					
	/Daytime B	7	1	7	Jan. 7-Mar. 7, 1975	59
	/Breakfast	14	2	7	Jan. 7-Mar. 7, 1975	118
		4	1	4	Mar. 8-Mar. 11, 1975	4
	Malay/PE A Time	3	1	3	Jan. 7-Feb. 12, 1975	18
					Feb. 22-Mar. 9, 1975	6
	/Breakfast	7	1	7	Jan. 7-Mar. 12, 1975	64
	/A Time	7	1	7	Jan. 7-Feb. 20, 1975	63
	/Daytime B	3	1	3	Jan. 8-Feb. 16, 1975	18
					Feb. 23-Mar. 9, 1975	6

Table 34 (continued)

Medium	Language/Type of Advertisement	Announcements per Week	Frequency Spots/Day	x Days/Week	Period	Total Spot Announcements
	Tamil/Breakfast	3	1	3	Jan. 7-Feb. 16, 1975	18
					Feb. 22-Mar. 9, 1975	6
		4	1	4	Mar. 11-Mar. 17, 1975	18
	/Daytime B	3	1	3	Jan. 7-Feb. 16, 1975	18
					Feb. 22-Mar. 9, 1975	6
Total		80				603
Rediffusion	Chinese*	28	4	7	Jan. 1-Feb. 28, 1975	236
	English	14	2	7	Jan. 1-Feb. 28, 1975	118
Total		42				354
Total		**157**				**1,169**

Source: L. Lee 1976, pp. 33-33a.

Note: A & B refer to different time slots of the day with different advertising rates (charges).
*Rotated in Mandarin, Hokkien and Cantonese.

Subsequently, it was taken on tour to 20 community centers in different parts of Singapore, drawing additional attendance of more than 21,000 people, and bringing the message to the people. In 1970, exhibitions were organized at Pulau Tekong and Pulau Ubin (two offshore islands) and Kampong Chai Chee (John 1976, p. 46).

In 1972, a massive educational and publicity campaign was arranged, with a committee set up to include representatives from a total of 22 ministries, boards, and organizations. Detailed briefs of activities were drawn up for each organization, and the extent of participation by each organization was discussed with its representatives. A ten-day exhibition was held at the Singapore Conference Hall, and again was followed by a "mobile" tour of 13 selected community centers scattered throughout the island. A total of 21,700 people attended at the Conference Hall, and a further 8,000 were attracted to the small exhibits at the community centers (John 1976, p. 46).

The emphasis on exhibitions was aimed to bring the message home to the people by way of pictures, illustrations, signs, and other symbols. At each exhibition location, pamphlets were distributed, demonstrations given, and clinical and nonclinical staff made available to answer questions and give directions for further services.

Talks and Discussions

The SFPPB arranges and accepts requests for talks on family planning. Such talks are often supplemented with slides and filmlets and are given readily to the army, police, community centers, schools, commercial firms, clubs, unions, and private organizations upon request. Since 1967, a special education program has been extended to the industrial and factory sector, consisting of a series of film shows and lectures-cum-demonstrations in the various languages/dialects. The purposes are to increase the level of knowledge regarding family planning, and to motivate and educate workers to seek family planning services.

Similarly, a Family Planning Advisory Service to newlyweds is provided once a week through regular public lectures in three languages (English, Mandarin, and Malay). A family planning worker at the Registry of Marriage issues invitations to these lectures to all couples getting married.

The main advantage of public talks is the ability to reach the target population through languages they understand. Speakers are trained and qualified staff or experts, work with slides and other visual media. Meeting audiences of various sizes, they can adapt to questions and queries, and encourage two-way communication. For the audience, the talks are a concentrated form of indoctrination and the attention given to this mode of persuasion is generally high.

This form of communication has been successful partly because of the small area of Singapore. A small group of trained personnel can be ready to travel to any part of the republic upon request. Two or three such talks may be arranged with the same group of personnel if there is a need. Even more significant is the cooperation and support given by various organizations because of the general awareness and support of the family planning program. Requests and arrangements for such talks are thus often made by labor unions, community centers, schools, and similar organizations.

Interpersonal Communication

Face-to-Face Communication

The most effective means of informing and educating the public is probably personal communication. Activities in this category include postpartum and postabortal contact services, in which every woman who delivers a child or who has an abortion in a government hospital is encouraged to accept family planning by a trained midwife. The service claims to be very effective from the psychological viewpoint.

Interpersonal communication also occurs in the Maternal and Child Health (MCH) Clinics when a mother comes for an antenatal check-up or brings her child for immunization. According to John (1976, p. 48), the quality of the clinical services provided has attracted patients from all sectors of the population. "These satisfied clients have acted as excellent diffusion agents to spread word of the facilities available as well as of the low cost of supplies available." (John 1976, p. 48). Home visits by staff nurses and social workers were initiated during 1972 in such selected areas as rural kampongs, city slums, and the Housing and Development Board's one-room apartments.

Community leaders such as MPs also carry out home visits to promote family planning, especially during the family planning campaigns.

Telephone Information Service

The most recent innovation by the SFPPB has been the installation of a telephone information service (TIS) in March 1974, to provide the population with a convenient means of obtaining immediate and reliable information on any matter related to family planning. Manned by six doctors and two nurses, this service provides an open channel for feedback from interested individuals who may have been motivated or persuaded by family planning messages from other sources. Calls may be made at any convenient time and with full protection of privacy. It is interesting, from the viewpoint of communication strategy, that the availability of the TIS had to be publicized widely over the mass media and through interpersonal communication. In 1974 and 1975, two campaigns were carried out for this purpose. Since then, most family planning publicity media carry both family planning slogans and the "Ring 538766" message.

The first campaign lasted from March 18, 1974 to August 4, 1974, and the second from December 30, 1974 to May 31, 1975. Some details about the use of mass media in these campaigns have been presented earlier in this section. According to the study by L. Lee (1976), a total of 595 telephone inquiries were received during the first campaign. After the introduction of fresh publicity in January 1975, telephone inquiries totaled 5,147 for the second campaign period (L. Lee 1976, p. 13). Lee observed that,

> Throughout the study period, the number of telephone calls was proportionate to the intensity of publicity over mass media. The average number of calls per day increased when more mass media channels and/or more frequent advertising was employed and fell substantially when mass media advertising stopped altogether. (1976, p. 13)

Comparing the effectiveness of different mass media, we found the newspaper to be the most effective in that it attracted the most calls per advertisement. Next in effectiveness was television, then radio, Rediffusion, and lastly cinema. This was also found to be the order of cost-effectiveness for the various mass media (L. Lee 1976, p. 29).

Other Promotional Media

Posters

The SFPPB also makes extensive use of posters with simple family planning messages prepared in different official languages. These posters are placed in public government offices, schools, hospitals, and bus stops all over the island.

Banners

Banners are also displayed along the street or across footbridges to attract the attention of both motorists and pedestrians. They are used only during campaign periods.

Bus Panels and Car Stickers

Other "traffic media" used to display the messages of planning are bus panels and car stickers. The SFPPB pays for advertisements on panels in both the interior and the exterior of the buses. In the 1975 TIS campaign, a total of 220 panels were displayed on buses plying routes through the most densely populated areas in order to obtain the maximum exposure (L. Lee 1976, p. 36). Car stickers were distributed free to motorists during the campaign period. Both bus panels and car stickers are characterized by their mobile quality; each has the potential of traveling over long distances to carry the message to a more varied and widely distributed audience.

Postmarks

With the cooperation of the Postal Services Department, postmarks bearing family planning messages were used on letters during campaigns, with the prospects of reaching thousands of households every day. Similarly, Telecommunication Authority of Singapore helped at the time of the campaigns by making recorded announcements about family planning in the "time of the day" service. Both the Postal Department and Telecom provide similar services to other national campaigns.

Other publicity media used by the SFPPB as "remembrance items" are calendars, ball-point pens, key chains, shopping bags, and telephone book advertisements.

Review of SFPPB Communication Planning

The family planning communication program in Singapore makes use of a combination of types of communication channels, especially in recent years (see Table 35). The strategy fits the classical diffusion model (Rogers 1967) in that mass communication is applied to create awareness and interpersonal communication is applied for acceptance and adoption among the target group.

As far as the mix of this multimedia approach is concerned, there do not seem to be any hard and fast rules regarding the exact balance of these channels of communication. According to John (1976, p. 63), the organization of communication strategies of the SFPPB is still on an "ad hoc basis" rather than on a long-term plan, because such a practice seems relevant in Singapore's case due to two factors.

> Firstly, the relatively small population of Singapore required that the social norm of a 2-child family should not become permanent, lest there would be a negative population growth; secondly, a more flexible communication programme could adjust to the urgency of the situation. (John 1976, p. 63)

In an interview, the head of the IEC Unit explained that the mixture and proportion of investment in each of the mass communication channels is based largely on a working model, a strategy that has been tried and found to have worked. It was also emphasized that the choice of how much to invest in a particular channel of communication is very much guided by research.

The contribution of the Research and Evaluation Unit is similarly emphasized by the SFPPB leadership. Wan and Loh (forthcoming) emphasize that such findings have contributed positively to decision making at various levels of policy formulation and program implementation: "Findings such as those on the effectiveness of various forms of mass-media publicity channels have influenced decisions on their use." It should be noted that the Research and Evaluation Unit has in recent years assumed responsibility for pretesting publicity materials, such as posters and pamphlets, and for evaluation of seminars and training courses.

Another characteristic of the family planning communication activities is that they involve very active support and commitment from both government and nongovernment organizations throughout the society. As we have

Table 35

Media Used in Family Planning Publicity, 1949–1975

Year	Press	Radio/Re-diffusion	Posters	Films/Slides	Television	Pamphlets	Exhibition
1949							
1950							
1951				+			
1952	+	+	+			+	
1953	+					+	
1954	+			+		+	
1955	+		+			+	
1956	+	+				+	+
1957	+	+		+		+	+
1958	+	+		+			+
1959	+	+	+	+			
1960	+	+	+			+	+
1961	+	+					+
1962							+
1963		+			+	+	
1964	+	+		+	+	+	
1965	+		+	+		+	+
1966	+	+	+		+	+	
1967		+	+	+	+	+	+
1968		+		+	+		
1969	+	+	+		+	+	+
1970	+	+	+	+	+	+	+
1971				+		+	
1972		+	+	+	+	+	+
1973	+	+	+	+	+	+	+
1974	+	+	+	+	+	+	+

Source: L. Lee 1974, p. 41.

shown, interorganizational ties play a very important part in the implementation of communication activities, because of the strong and effective political control of the PAP government through its overall organizational network.

Despite the active programs being carried out in Singapore, the number of personnel in the SFPPB directly in charge of implementing communication activities is surprisingly small. From the SFPPB *Tenth Annual Report, 1975* (p. 23), we find only three communication officers in the IEC Unit and one communication officer in the Training Unit, out of a total staff of 171 on the Board in 1975. It is likely that planning and implementation of communication activities are often done with the assistance of experts and resources from external sources.

9

Summary and Conclusion

As a compact urban society, Singapore is characterized by a set of well-developed communication systems. There are eleven daily newspapers, published in five languages, serving the linguistically diverse population. The average daily circulation was estimated to be 477,000 in 1976, giving a circulation rate of 209 papers per 1,000 population. Radio and television services are operated by the government under the Ministry of Culture. There are four AM radio channels plus an FM stereo service and a short-wave service, and two television channels. Four official languages are used in radio and television broadcasting. A balance between development and nondevelopment-oriented programs is maintained. In addition, a privately operated cable audio broadcasting service, Rediffusion, is available and quite popular among the Chinese population. There are at present 72 cinemas with a total seating capacity of 63,000, averaging 27 seats per 1,000 population.

Audience analysis has revealed that the Singapore population is highly exposed to mass media, as is typical in a highly urbanized society. Newspapers, television, and, to a lesser extent, radio are important sources of information for the population, and television and movies have become probably the most popular forms of entertainment in the island-republic.

The Singapore government gives high priority to the development of telecommunications (telephone, telex, and telegraph systems, and the satellite communication network), since these are considered the basic infrastructure for economic and social development in a country that depends so much on international communication. In terms of per capita use and capital investment in telecommunication, Singapore is among the highest in the world.

The political leaders of Singapore perceive communication media as powerful instruments to be properly controlled or guided to play a positive role in social development. Some constraints and censorship are viewed as necessary because Singapore is vulnerable to external influences, whether intended or unintended. Ethnic issues and communist ideology are considered to be sensitive areas on which restrictive measures should be imposed. Laws and statutes are therefore enacted to place the various communication systems under direct or indirect government supervision. Radio, television, and telecommunication systems, as well as the postal service, are directly owned and operated by the government as part of the government bureaucracy. Privately owned newspapers, magazines, and cinemas are allowed to operate under legal proscriptions. According to the political leaders, such constraints are necessary because of the unique social-political situation in Singapore at its present stage of development.

Singapore is known to be a planned society, and its planning framework is, in general, a centralized one. But there is no centralized national planning agency. Development planning in Singapore is characterized by flexibility, efficiency, and pragmatism, making Singapore highly adaptive and responsive to changing situations. Such pragmatic strategy is necessary since many external factors influence Singapore's economy and society. On the other hand, such a pragmatic planning approach works well in Singapore because of the relative simplicity of the economic structure, the continuity of political leadership, and the efficiency of the government bureaucracy.

At the level of national communication planning, infrastructure planning is done by the ministries and departments that are involved with communication elements. Planning involving communication facilities or technology is either submitted as part of annual budget requests or subsumed under general development planning. The processes of communication infrastructure planning do not differ from those of other types of development project planning.

In communication operation planning, each relevant division or department is responsible for the operation of the communication elements under its charge. Through its connections with mass media, the Ministry of Culture is responsible for overall coordination to make sure that government communication policy guidelines are followed.

To understand the role of the communication sector in social development, an analysis of communication planning at the institutional level has been carried out. Our case study of Radio Television Singapore (RTS) shows how the programs are planned and arranged to maintain a balance between development-oriented and nondevelopment-oriented contents. Within RTS, a Central Production Unit is responsible for the production of programs relevant to current affairs and issues regarding nation-building. Presently, informational and educational programs occupy about one-third of radio and television transmission hours. While imported TV programs are usually entertaining in nature and highly popular with the audience, careful censorship is imposed by RTS in the selection of imported TV series and films.

Radio and television in Singapore follow closely the policy of multilingualism. Since there are four channels serving audiences in four official languages, the distribution of radio airtime is relatively even. But such balanced distribution of television time is not possible because imported programs are more readily available in the English and Chinese languages and are very popular. This situation is slightly improved by subtitling and dubbing programs in several languages.

RTS plays an important role in promoting and supporting government development projects. Activities of these projects may appear in newscasts or in programs produced by the Central Production Unit, such as *Forum*, *Opinion*, and documentaries. Spot announcements and filmlets are also used to promote public campaigns, as are development messages inserted in regular women's and children's programs, for example.

At the project planning level, we have presented a case study of family planning communication in Singapore to illustrate how different communication channels are used to promote the norms and practices of family planning. The Singapore Family Planning and Population Board (SFPPB) makes extensive use of mass media in combination with group communication (exhibitions, talks, and discussions) and interpersonal communication (postpartum and postabortal consultation, home visits, and telephone service). The combination of various communication channels is especially revealing.

Family planning communication activities in Singapore are supported by a well-coordinated organizational network linking government ministries, schools, unions, and community centers. Skillfully used by government leaders, this network provides a basic structure whereby the population can be reached and mobilized to support and participate in programs for national development.

Singapore society is unique in many ways. Geographically, it is small in size and lacking natural resources and a hinterland. Yet it has a deep-water harbor located at a strategic position between the South China Sea and the Indian Ocean. The island is densely populated, with a diverse ethnic composition. There are four official languages and many dialects in use, but none of them can be considered a *lingua franca*. In our case study on communication policy and planning in Singapore, we found that all the above factors, as well as the political/economic conditions of the society, are closely related to one another and to the development of the communication system and the policy planning patterns.

The compact urban context of Singapore means easy reach, easy control, and a high level of media exposure of the population. There is no distinction between national and local governments, nor between industrial and agricultural sectors, reflecting the relatively small scale of the economy and simple government structure. All these make planning easy and coordination possible.

Singapore's economy stresses international trade, manufacturing, shipping, and tourism. More recently, the government has been trying to develop Singapore into a "global city" to serve the region and the world as a financial and banking center and a consultant service center. All such economic activities rely much on efficient communication facilities. Development in the communication sector, especially of telecommunication systems, is therefore given priority as the infrastructure for economic development.

Due to its ethnic and linguistic diversity, and the need to maintain ethnic harmony and communicative integration, a policy of multiracialism and multilingualism is adopted. The unique practice of providing mass media contents in four official languages makes the structure of the communication sector rather complicated. For instance, special efforts are made to balance radio and television transmission hours among the four official languages. The implementation of the multilingual policy is necessary but costly, and results in some redundancy in content and duplication of effort. Obviously, this practice consumes a considerable share of the limited financial and manpower resources available to Singapore's communication sector.

As an ethnically plural society, Singapore relies on its economic prosperity for its political survival as a sovereign state. In turn, its economic development depends on internal ethnic harmony and social stability. Yet, because of the complex ethnic composition, Singapore is vulnerable to foreign instigation and communal strife. These factors, according to government leaders, make it justifiable for the government to impose regulatory constraints on communication systems. Communication media must not fall into the wrong hands or be abused to disrupt social stability. Moreover, they must be properly used for political socialization and nation-building. To the leaders of Singapore, freedom of the press is not absolute. The uniqueness of Singapore's local conditions justifies contraints on such freedom when the survival of the society is at stake.

The communication pattern in Singapore is characterized by a largely one-way flow from the leadership to the masses with government and media people at various levels serving a gatekeeping function. Under the circumstances, the mass media often fail to be effective channels for political articulation and participation by the general public, although they have played an important role in supporting national development in Singapore.

Appendix 1

The Communication Network in Singapore

The Press (1976):
11 Daily Newspapers in 5 Languages
Circulation: 477,000
209 per 1,000 Population

Radio (1978):
4 AM Channels in 4 Languages, 1 FM,
1 Short-Wave Service
Licenses: 410,532
176 Licenses per 1,000 Population

Rediffusion Services (1978):
93,175 Subscribers
40 Sets per 1,000 Population

TV (1978):
2 Channels in Singapore, 4 Languages
Licenses: 353,248
151 Licenses per 1,000 Population

Cinema (1978):
72 Cinemas
Seating Capacity: 67,000
29 Seats per 1,000 Population
Annual Attendance: 44,676,000

Post (1977):
62 Post Offices
49 Postal Agencies
520,000 Mail Articles per Day

Telephone (1978):
327,000 Lines
460,000 Phones
197 per 1,000 Population

International Telephone (1976):
184 Countries
1,077,000 Calls

Telex (1976):
165 Countries
2,240 Subscribers
2,330,000 Calls

Telegrams (1976):
8,053,000 Sent

Satellite Communication Network:
Intelsat
Marisat
Inmarsat

Appendix 2

Breakdown of Television Singapore Programs by Language, Type of Program, and Location of Production

1. Breakdown of Programming

	Total %	Local Productions %	Foreign Productions %
Chinese	24.4	37.6	17.0
Malay	11.2	29.6	0.8
Tamil	8.3	16.7	3.6
English	56.0	16.1	78.5

2. Breakdown by Program Categories

	%		%
Education/Information	29.0	Westerns	4.0
Feature Films	18.3	Mystery	2.9
Drama	17.2	Sports	2.6
Music and Musical Variety	7.8	Daytime Serials	2.6
Comedy	4.5	Adventures	2.2
Children/Youth	4.3	Quizzes and Games	0.4
Cartoons	4.3		

3. Breakdown of Imported Programs

	%		%
Drama	26	Sports	6
Education/Information	15	Daytime Serials	6
Comedy	10	Adventure	5
Cartoons	9	Children/Youth	4
Westerns	9	Music and Musical Variety	3
Mystery	6	Quizzes and Games	1

4. Breakdown of Local Productions by Language Stream (percent)

	Chinese	Malay	Tamil	English	Total
News and Newsreels (Educ/Info)	6.5	6.0	6.0	8.5	27.0
Magazine Format (Educ/Info)	6.9	4.0	2.5	4.2	17.6
Public Affairs (Educ/Info)	8.2	5.8	1.1	1.8	16.9
Drama	6.5	6.0	2.2	—	14.7
Music and Musical Variety	4.9	4.2	2.0	—	11.1
Arts/Cultural	1.6	1.3	1.6	1.6	6.1
Youth/Children	3.1	2.2	1.3	—	6.6

Source: Malolos 1977, pp. 62-63.

Appendix 3

RTS's Requirements for Advertising Material (Section B)

The Broadcasting Department will not accept advertising material which:

1. Contains exaggerated or superlative claims or misleading statements.
2. Disparages, directly or inferentially, any other product, service, organisation or person.
3. Claims that a product can be used to treat any condition which properly requires professional medical attention.
4. Tends to endanger health or character; or to offend the proprieties or ethics generally observed by the community.
5. Utilises disturbing or irritating sound effects; employs sound effects merely as devices for attracting attention; employs any techniques liable to mislead or alarm listeners; or contains any wordage or effects which closely approximate the standard Broadcasting Department procedures.
6. Offers to diagnose, treat or advise on any ailment by correspondence.
7. Leads listeners to conclude that they are suffering from a particular ailment.
8. Imitates or too closely approximates the trade names or catch-phrases used by another organisation.
9. Describes graphically or repellently any physical condition or function; or simulates the symptoms or effects of any ailment.
10. Urges children to request adults to buy a product not of intrinsic juvenile appeal; or persuades juveniles to make unsuitable or costly purchases.
11. Contains derogatory remarks or innuendos about any person or organisation; criticises directly or inferentially the Government of any country.
12. Attempts to exploit any abnormal national or international events or conditions.
13. Makes irreverent reference to any name, incident, or concept, of religious significance.
14. Contains statements or suggestions which may offend the religious, racial, political, or sentimental susceptibilities of any section of the community.
15. Advertises matter which is barred from the mails as fraudulent, deceptive, or objectionable.
16. Refers to any activity which constitutes a breach of the law.
17. Publicises any form of speculative finance, intended to promote the purchase of specific stocks and shares.
18. Tends to subvert or disparage law and order, adult authority, or moral standards.
19. Introduces dramatisation other than straight two-voice announcing into spoken copy.
20. Contains recognisable imitations or parodies of prominent vocal artistes.
21. Comprises a public notice of death or funeral arrangements or advertises a firm of funeral directors or monumental masons.
22. Contains terms, words, or subject matter not generally considered acceptable in polite conversation.
23. Is considered inappropriate tq the programme or session in which it is intended for broadcast.

24. Publicises controversial activities or opinions. Copy that deals with a controversial subject, or that is likely to involve the Broadcasting Department in a dispute of a public or private nature is not acceptable. Meetings on a controversial subject may be advertised on the same basis as political meetings.

The Broadcasting Department reserves the right to require the withdrawal of previously accepted material if, in its opinion, such withdrawal appears desirable.

Source: Association of Accredited Advertising Agents, 1977, p. 49.

References

Association of Accredited Advertising Agents.

1977 *1976/1977 Media Directory, Singapore, Malaysia and Brunei.* Singapore.

Bellows, T.

1970 *The People's Action Party, Singapore: Emergence of a Dominant Party System.* New Haven: Yale University, Southeast Asian Studies.

Benveniste, Guy.

1968 "Towards a Sociology of National Development Planning." *Journal of Developing Areas* 3:27–36.

Burns, Peter Lourie.

1957 "The English Language Newspapers of Singapore, 1915–1951." Unpublished paper, University of Singapore, Department of History.

Byrd, Cecil K.

1970 *Books in Singapore.* Singapore: Chopman.

Chan, Heng Chee.

1971 *Singapore: The Politics of Survival, 1965–1967.* Singapore: Oxford University Press.

1975 "Politics in an Administrative State: Where Has the Politics Gone?" In *Trends in Singapore*, edited by C. M. Seah, pp. 51–68. Singapore: Institute of Southeast Asian Studies.

Chen, Mong-hock.

1967 *The Early Chinese Newspapers of Singapore, 1881–1912.* Singapore: University of Malaya Press.

Chen, Peter S.J.

1973 *National Reports on a Comparative Study of Husband-Wife Communication and Practice of Family Planning, Report 1: Singapore.* Bangkok: ESCAP. Mimeographed.

1976–1977 "Public Housing and Urban Development in Singapore." *Journal of the Singapore Institute of Planners* 6(1):59–71.

1978 "The Power Elite in Singapore." In *Studies in ASEAN Sociology*, edited by Peter Chen and Hans Evers, pp. 73–82. Singapore: Chopman.

Chen, Peter S.J. and Fawcett, James T., eds.

forthcoming* *Public Policy and Population Change in Singapore.* New York: Population Council.

Chen, Peter S.J. and Kuo, Eddie C.Y.

1978 *Mass Media and Communication Patterns in Singapore.* Singapore: AMIC.

*While this volume was in press, this book was published in 1979.

Chong, Hoi Kong.
1977 "The Study of Language Maintenance and Shift in Singapore as a Multilingual Society." Unpublished project report. Singapore: Regional Language Centre.

Chong, Li Choy.
1974 "Social Planning Strategies in Southeast Asia—Current Approaches to Planned Development in Four Nations." Master's thesis, University of Singapore.

Department of Statistics.
1976 *Yearbook of Statistics, Singapore, 1975/1976.* Singapore.

Far Eastern Economic Review.
1976 *Asia 1976 Yearbook.* Hong Kong.

Fawcett, James T. and Chen, Peter S.J.
forthcoming* "Public Policy and Population Change: An Appraisal of the Singapore Experience." In *Public Policy and Population Change in Singapore*, edited by Chen and Fawcett, pp. 243-258.

Feliciano, Gloria D.
1976 "Communication and Development in Southeast Asia, 1964-1974." In *Communication and Change: The Last Ten Years—and the Next,* edited by W. Schramm and D. Lerner, pp. 191-203. Honolulu: The University Press of Hawaii.

Government Printing Office.
1957 *Report of the Committee Appointed to Examine the Possibility of Introducing Television in Singapore.* Singapore.

Hon, Sui Sen.
1973 "Development Priorities—Past, Present and Future." In *Toward Tomorrow: Essays on Development and Social Transformation in Singapore,* edited by the Singapore National Trade Union Congress (NTUC), pp. 17-23. Singapore: NTUC.

John, Jacintha.
1976 "The Administration of Family Planning Programmes in Singapore." Unpublished paper, University of Singapore, Department of Political Science.

Kanayson, A.
1956 "The Newspapers of Singapore, 1824-1914." Unpublished paper, University of Singapore, Department of History.

Koh, Edgar.
1973 "Whither RTS?" *New Nation* June 18-20. Singapore.

Kuo, Eddie C.Y.
1974 "Language Status and Literacy Trends in a Multilingual Society—Singapore." *RELC Journal* 5:1-5.

1976 "A Sociolinguistic Profile." In *Singapore: Society in Transition,* edited by Riaz Hassan, pp. 134–148. Kuala Lumpur: Oxford University Press.

1977a "The Status of English Language in Singapore: A Sociolinguistic Analysis." In *The English Language in Singapore,* edited by William Crewe, pp. 10–33. Singapore: Eastern Universities Press.

1977b "Language, Nationhood, and Communication Planning: The Case of a Multilingual Society." In *Perspectives in Communication Policy and Planning,* edited by Rahim and Middleton, pp. 319–336.

1978 "Multilingualism and Mass Media Communication in Singapore." *Asian Survey* 18 (October):1067–1083.

Lee, John A.R.
1976 *Towards Realistic Communication Policies: Recent Trends and Ideas Compiled and Analysed.* Reports and Papers on Communication, No. 76. Paris: Unesco.

Lee, Luisa.
1976 "A Brief Survey of Mass Media Communications in Family Planning in Singapore with Particular Reference to the Singapore Family Planning and Population Board's Telephone Information Service." Master's thesis, University of Singapore.

Lee, Soo Ann.
1973 "Singapore." In *Development Planning in Southeast Asia: Role of the University,* edited by Y.H. Yip, pp. 1–72. Singapore: Regional Institute of Higher Education and Development.

Lim, Lena U. Wen; Lui-Tan, Kwan Siu; and Foo, Choy Hung.
1975 "Information Imbalance: The Singapore Scene." Paper presented at AMIC regional conference on "Information Imbalance in Asia," April 1975, at Kandy, Sri Lanka. Mimeographed.

Malolos, Maria T.I.
1977 "Communication Policy and Planning for National Integration: Case Studies of Singapore and Guam." Master's thesis, University of Hawaii.

Ministry of Culture.
1973 *RTS: From Many Cultures One Voice.* Singapore.

1975–1977 *Singapore: Facts and Pictures.* Singapore.

1977 *Singapore '76.* Singapore.

***The Mirror.* Singapore.**

***Nanyang Siang Pao.* Singapore.**

Neo, Lay Tin.
1978 "Content Analysis of Letters to the Editor: An Exploratory Study." Unpublished paper, University of Singapore, Department of Sociology.

***New Nation.* Singapore.**

Pang, Eng Fong.
forthcoming* "Public Policy on Population, Employment, and Immigration." In *Public Policy and Population Change in Singapore*, edited by Chen and Fawcett, pp. 205–215.

Rahim, Syed A.
1977 "Introduction: The Scope of Communication Policy and Planning Research." In *Perspectives in Communication Policy and Planning*, edited by Rahim and Middleton, pp. 5–24.

1978 "The Organizational and Methodological Aspects of Communication Planning." In *Planning Methods, Models, and Organization: A Review Study for Communication Policy Making and Planning*, by Syed A. Rahim, Donald McL. Lamberton, Dan Wedemeyer, John Holmstrom, John Middleton, and Barclay Hudson, pp. 1–12. Honolulu: East-West Center.

Rahim, Syed A. and Middleton, John, eds.
1977 *Perspectives in Communication Policy and Planning*. Communication Monographs No. 3. Honolulu: East-West Center.

Rogers, Everett M.
1967 *Diffusion of Innovation.* New York: Wiley and Sons.

1973 *Communication Strategies for Family Planning.* New York: The Free Press.

1976 "Communication and Development: The Passing of the Dominant Paradigm." *Communication Research* 3:213–240.

Seah, Linda.
1976 "Economic Planning in Singapore." *Prospect* 8(5/6):18–19; 8(7/8): 22–23.

***Sin Chew Jit Poh.* Singapore.**

Singapore Family Planning and Population Board.
1975a *Family Planning and Population Board, Paper No. 34.* Singapore.

1975b *SFPPB Tenth Annual Report, 1975.* Singapore.

Singapore Legislative Assembly Debates.
Singapore: Government Printing Office.

Singapore Parliamentary Debates.
Singapore: Government Printing Office.

Sommerlad, L.
1975 *National Communication Systems: Some Policy Issues and Options.* Paris: Unesco Press.

***Straits Times.* Singapore.**

***Sunday Times.* Singapore.**

Thomson, George G.
1974 "Communication's Tasks in a City State." *Media Asia* 1(1):23-29.

Wan, Fook Kee and Loh, Margaret T.F.
forthcoming* "Fertility Policies and the National Family Planning and Population Programme." In *Public Policy and Population Change in Singapore,* edited by Chen and Fawcett, pp. 97-108.

Waterston, Albert.
1965 *Development Planning: Lessons of Experience.* Baltimore, Maryland: Johns Hopkins Press.

Wee, Serene W.K.
1977 "Use of Mass Media in Mass Campaigns." Unpublished paper, University of Singapore, Department of Sociology.